# Black Widow

A play

# Paul Thain

Samuel French — London
New York - Toronto - Hollywood

Copyright © 1996 by Paul Thain
All Rights Reserved

*BLACK WIDOW* is fully protected under the copyright laws of the British Commonwealth, including Canada, the United States of America, and all other countries of the Copyright Union. All rights, including professional and amateur stage productions, recitation, lecturing, public reading, motion picture, radio broadcasting, television and the rights of translation into foreign languages are strictly reserved.

ISBN 978-0-573-01727-8

www.samuelfrench.co.uk

www.samuelfrench.com

---

For Amateur Production Enquiries

United Kingdom and World excluding north america

plays@samuelfrench.co.uk

020 7255 4302/01

Each title is subject to availability from Samuel French, depending upon country of performance.

---

CAUTION: Professional and amateur producers are hereby warned that BLACK WIDOW is subject to a licensing fee. Publication of this play does not imply availability for performance. Both amateurs and professionals considering a production are strongly advised to apply to the appropriate agent before starting rehearsals, advertising, or booking a theatre. A licensing fee must be paid whether the title is presented for charity or gain and whether or not admission is charged.

The Professional Rights in this play are controlled by Casarotto Ramsay Ltd, 12 Noel St, Soho, London W1F 8GQ.

No one shall make any changes in this title for the purpose of production. No part of this book may be reproduced, stored in a retrieval system, or transmitted in any form, by any means, now known or yet to be invented, including mechanical, electronic, photocopying, recording, videotaping, or otherwise, without the prior written permission of the publisher. No one shall upload this title, or part of this title, to any social media websites.

The right of Paul Thain to be identified as author of this work has been asserted in accordance with Section 77 of the Copyright, Designs and Patents Act 1988.

## CHARACTERS

**Rector**
**Lady Cressida Arlington**
**Emily Arlington**
**Chief Inspector Aubrey Dachett**
**Lady Isobel Arlington**
**Mabel**
**Dorothy**
**Richard Harker**
**Mrs Hodge**
**Voice**
**Dr Shawcross**
**Inspector Eaton**
**Sergeant Charlton**

The action of the play takes place in the house of Lady Cressida Arlington and in various locations around it

Time — Winter 1909

## AUTHOR'S NOTE

No set is required, but the rear of the stage must be raised slightly and should include two, perhaps three, curved steps. Light and sound must be as sophisticated as resources allow, conjuring mood and atmosphere and facilitating fluid changes of scene. Several scenes are realized using only oil-lamps and candles.

The play can be performed by ten actors — four male, six female — if the Rector doubles as Voice and Inspector Eaton and Dr Shawcross doubles with Sergeant Charlton. Conversely, the cast can easily be increased to include extra mourners and guests.

For Jane

## ACT I

*Winter, 1909*

*We hear the sounds of a cold wind blowing and a church bell tolling as Lights slowly rise on Arlington Cemetery*

*Led by the Rector — reciting from his Book of Common Prayer — a procession of dark and veiled mourners enters and snakes its way c. The mourners are: Lady Cressida Arlington, in her thirties; her daughter Emily, who is in her mid-teens; Aubrey, a retired Police Inspector; two ageing spinster sisters, Mabel and Dorothy; Isobel, in her sixties, her arthritic hands gripping a walking-stick; Richard Harker, in his thirties; Mrs Hodge, the housekeeper, and finally Dr Shawcross, a Scot*

**Rector** I am the Resurrection and the Life. He that believeth in me, though he were dead, he shall live. Whosoever liveth and believeth in me shall never die.

*The mourners group around an imaginary open grave. To the Rector's right stand Cressida and Emily with, next to them, Aubrey, then Mabel and Dorothy. To the Rector's left stand Isobel with Richard Harker next to her, then Mrs Hodge and finally Dr Shawcross*

Behold, I show you a mystery ... We shall not all sleep. But we shall be changed.
**Emily** Into what? Changed into what?
**Cressida** Quiet.
**Rector** For the trumpet shall sound, and the Dead shall be raised. Man that is born of Woman hath but a short time to live and is full of Misery. He cometh up, and is cut down like a Flower. For in the midst of Life, we are in Death.

*Cressida steps forward and takes a handful of earth. This is mimed*

We therefore commit his body to the ground. Earth to earth, ashes to ashes ——

*Cressida releases earth into the grave*

— dust to dust ——

**Cressida** Emily ...
**Rector** — in the sure and certain hope of the Resurrection ——
**Emily** Do I have to?
**Cressida** Yes.
**Rector** — through our Lord Jesus Christ. Amen.
**Mourners** Amen ...

*Emily takes a handful of earth and stares into the grave, her fist closed tight*

**Cressida** Emily ...
**Emily** Will this happen to me?
**Isobel** For heaven's sake!
**Aubrey** Isobel ...
**Emily** Will it? Will it happen to me?
**Isobel** Questions, questions, all the time questions — even now.
**Cressida** Emily, please.

*Emily releases her earth. Cressida ushers her further downstage*

*The Mourners repeat the ritual, then formally line up to offer condolences to Cressida. Dr Shawcross takes Cressida's hand*

**Doctor** My dear Cressida ... what can I say? Poor Toby — a tragedy, no other word, a terrible, terrible tragedy.

*Mrs Hodge rushes up, bobs a curtsy, fighting back her tears*

**Mrs Hodge** Oh, ma'am ... all his life. I knew him all his life.
**Doctor** (*smoothing her hand*) Never forget ... if there's anything I can do, anything at all ——
**Mrs Hodge** It seems like only yesterday we was — I'm sorry, I can't help it.
**Cressida** (*rescuing her hand*) Thank you for coming, Doctor. Hadn't you better be getting back, Mrs Hodge?
**Mrs Hodge** (*bobbing*) Of course, ma'am. Sorry, ma'am.

*She hurries off*

*During the following Aubrey reaches Cressida*

*Isobel begins to approach, escorted by Richard, painfully picking their way with her stick*

**Isobel** You seem to have made an excellent recovery?

Act I                                                                      3

**Richard**  Yes, I'm much better, your ladyship.
**Isobel**  With Toby being that much older, I suppose he —— (*She stops, resting on her stick*) Don't worry. Sometimes I get a little breathless.

*Aubrey with Cressida and Emily*

**Aubrey**  Dear oh dear ... life can seem so cruel. At least it's all behind you now.
**Emily**  Will he be there yet?
**Aubrey**  Beg pardon?
**Emily**  Papa. Will he be in Heaven now?
**Aubrey**  I dare say. Having a good old chin-wag, I shouldn't wonder. Don't you think, Cressida?
**Cressida**  Yes, I expect so.
**Emily**  But only if he's judged worthy, only if God finds him worthy.
**Cressida**  Emily ...
**Emily**  Isn't that right, Uncle Aubrey?
**Aubrey**  Your father was the most righteous of men, I'm sure God ——
**Emily**  Otherwise he'll burn in Hell. He'll be sent to Hell and burn for all eternity. That's what happens to the wicked, to the sinful. That's why we must always be good.
**Cressida**  Emily Arlington, that is quite enough.
**Emily**  Yes, Mama.

*Richard approaches with Isobel. He nods, stands awkwardly, fumbling with his hat*

**Richard**  I don't quite know what to say.
**Cressida**  Then perhaps it's best you say nothing.
**Richard**  I wasn't even sure I should come.
**Cressida**  My husband considered you a friend, Mr Harker.
**Richard**  What I meant was ——
**Cressida**  I know what you meant. No-one blames you, least of all me. Please don't torment yourself. Toby wouldn't want that.
**Richard**  No. No, he wouldn't.
**Isobel**  (*shivering against the cold*) It's no use, the blood's too thin. Mr Harker — would you be so kind as to see me to my carriage?
**Richard**  Of course, your ladyship.

*Richard leads Isobel off*

**Aubrey**  (*as they go*) Poor fellow, must be dreadful.

*Dorothy and Mabel bustle up*

**Mabel** You don't remember us, do you?
**Aubrey** (*heading off*) See you back at the house, Cressida.
**Mabel** Mabel and Dorothy. I'm Mabel ——
**Dorothy** — and I'm Dorothy.
**Mabel** We're cousins ...
**Dorothy** Cousins of Toby.
**Mabel** Twice removed. From Bridlington.
**Dorothy** Bridlington.
**Mabel** You came to Sunday tea seven years ago. August, late August.
**Dorothy** Only it rained and the summer house leaked.
**Mabel** Uncle George was there.
**Dorothy** You must remember Uncle George?
**Mabel** No matter, my dear, I'm sure it'll come back. And this must be Emily? My, my ... how she's grown.
**Dorothy** Hasn't she grown?
**Mabel** Quite the young lady. And how are you, my dear?
**Dorothy** Yes, how are you?
**Emily** We've just buried Father. How do you suppose I am?
**Dorothy** Oh.
**Cressida** Emily!
**Emily** Well really, Mama — what a silly question.
**Dorothy** What I meant, what we meant, what we meant was ... that is to say ——
**Mabel** Do be quiet, Dorothy. Well said, Emily. Plain speaking and plain living, these are Arlington virtues, are they not?

*Distant thunder. The sky begins to darken. Cressida raises her eyes*

    Wouldn't you agree, Cressida?
**Cressida** It's going to rain.
**Mabel** Poor dear, you look exhausted.
**Cressida** I am rather. It's been a difficult time.
**Mabel** Be brave.
**Dorothy** Oh yes. Do be brave.
**Mabel** You won't always feel like this.
**Dorothy** Oh no, not at all, not at all. Time. Time can be a great ——
**Cressida** You're both very kind, but now I think I should like to be alone.
**Mabel** Of course, my dear. Dorothy ... and you, Emily. Now, now — come along.

*Mabel ushers Dorothy and Emily off during the following*

*Cressida moves upstage*

# Act I 5

Mama needs to be left with her grief.

*They go; the Rector, Aubrey and Dr Shawcross exit as well*

*Cressida now stands, head lowered, staring into the grave. The sound of the cold wind rises*

*The Lights slowly fade to Black-out and thunder rumbles closer*

*Dr Shawcross, Emily, Mabel, Dorothy, the Rector, Aubrey and Richard enter and join Cressida upstage*

*From the black, there is a huge crash; a shudder of white light reveals ——*

*Isobel, sitting hunched in a downstage chair. The shadowy figures of the mourners can be dimly perceived upstage*

**Isobel** (*muttering*) Gone, gone ... all gone ... all gone, dead and gone ...

*Dr Shawcross laughs in the dark*

*The Lights rise. As they do so, Isobel looks behind, calling to her dead son*

Toby? Toby ...?

*Dr Shawcross laughs again — and the shadowy figures upstage assume the identity of the mourners, Emily, Cressida, Dr Shawcross, Mabel, Dorothy, the Rector, Aubrey and Richard. Mrs Hodge weaves between them, serving sherry from a silver tray. Sandwiches are also being served. The conversations in the following sequence fade in and out and overlap*

*Emily approaches Isobel*

**Emily** Gran? Gran, it's me — Emily.
**Isobel** I thought ... for a moment I thought ...
**Aubrey** (*to Richard*) Revenge, passion, murder ——
**Isobel** Your father.
**Aubrey** — it's all there.
**Isobel** I was remembering your father.
**Aubrey** Sure to be a roaring success.

*Mrs Hodge approaches Cressida and the Rector*

**Mrs Hodge** (*bobbing*) Beggin' your pardon, ma'am. Cook wants to know how many for dinner?

*Mabel and Dorothy in conversation with Dr Shawcross*

**Dorothy** This is our third funeral this month.
**Mabel** No, no — our fourth.
**Dorothy** Fourth?
**Aubrey** Even thought of the title ——
**Mabel** For heaven's sake, Dorothy.
**Aubrey** — *An Inspector Recalls.*
**Mabel** First there was Mrs Eldridge ——
**Aubrey** Has a certain ring, don't you think?
**Dorothy** — then Major Pope.
**Mabel** Miss Spinks. Miss Spinks the schoolteacher, *then* Major Pope.
**Richard** I'm sorry?
**Aubrey** My memoirs ——
**Dorothy** So it must be our fourth.
**Aubrey** — *An Inspector Recalls.*
**Mabel** Of course it's our fourth.
**Aubrey** I was rather hoping you might help with a publisher ...?
**Richard** Aubrey, I run a village bookshop. I stack books and dust shelves, what possible influence ——
**Aubrey** Surely you must know someone? I mean it is your trade, your — your profession. And believe me, if you had the slightest inkling of the months and months of dedication and sheer hard ——
**Richard** I don't doubt it, but ——
**Aubrey** Dear boy ... I was rather relying on you.
**Emily** Wasn't it horrible?
**Richard** I'll see what I can do.
**Aubrey** Splendid!
**Emily** I didn't realize it would be so horrible.
**Isobel** Horrible? What's horrible?
**Emily** Being buried. Left to rot. You're old. Soon you'll be dead. Doesn't it scare you?
**Isobel** What!
**Emily** Doesn't it frighten you?
**Isobel** Wretched girl! There you go again!
**Emily** It frightens me.
**Isobel** Why can't you think before you speak?
**Emily** But I do. Gran, I always do.
**Isobel** Get out of my sight! Go on ... get away, get away!

*Emily retreats, wandering between the mourners, eavesdropping*

# Act I

**Mabel** And are you a married man, Doctor?
**Doctor** A widower these past five years.
**Mabel** Indeed? I'm so sorry.
**Dorothy** We're so sorry.
**Mabel** I'm sure there must be times when you find it very lonely?

*Emily moves on*

**Rector** As recent incumbent, I didn't know your husband terribly well, Lady Arlington, but I understand him to have been a God-fearing man of unusual zeal and, er ... conviction?
**Cressida** He held strong views, Rector. And frequently expressed them.
**Rector** So I believe. But we are all united in Christ, are we not? Which brings me to a rather important matter concerning —— (*he sees Emily*) Oh. Hallo ...
**Cressida** Say hallo to the Rector, Emily.
**Rector** Perhaps we're feeling a little shy, are we ...? Hm?
**Emily** Do you think it fitting for a man of God to drink alcohol?
**Rector** (*laughing*) Oh, I say.
**Cressida** Emily!
**Emily** Papa always said you were far too liberal.
**Rector** Did he now?
**Cressida** Emily!
**Rector** No, no, please — not on my account.

*Emily wanders away*

Mind you, she certainly seems to be her father's daughter.
**Aubrey** The Basingstoke Strangler. Now that was my true moment of glory. I was in all the papers. Oh yes. Pictures and everything.
**Doctor** Ay well, ladies ——
**Aubrey** National hero, no less.
**Doctor** — never forget, it comes to us all.
**Mabel** (*sourly*) Indeed ....
**Doctor** When your time's up, your time's up. None of us are immune.
**Mabel** Quite ...
**Dorothy** None of us.
**Doctor** Yet so few are prepared.
**Mabel** Indeed, quite so, Doctor. But do tell — what exactly happened?
**Rector** I was wondering if we might consider some kind of tribute to his memory? The refurbishment of the organ, perhaps?
**Mabel** We are cousins of the deceased, Dr Shawcross. We have travelled a great distance.

**Dorothy** Yes, a great, a very great ——
**Mabel** Surely we have a right to know?

*Dr Shawcross relents, huddles them together*

**Rector** As I recall our greatest poet once said, and I myself entirely agree: Music — music is the ——
**Mabel** Poison!
**Dorothy** Poison?

*A sudden lull — all eyes turn to Dr Shawcross*

**Doctor** No, no — food poisoning! Corned beef, a corned beef ——

*Dr Shawcross is at the centre of the sudden silence, and smiles woodenly. After a pause, conversation politely continues*

**Rector** ... suitably inscribed, of course. Nothing vulgar, ostentatious. Something plain and simple. A tasteful brass plaque, perhaps: "In loving memory of a dear, departed ——."

*Cressida laughs sadly*

**Cressida** Forgive me ... my ... my husband rarely approved of music.
**Rector** What? Not even in church?
**Cressida** I'm afraid he'd have considered an organ far too frivolous.
**Rector** Frivolous?
**Cressida** (*moving away*) Will you excuse me?
**Mabel** (*whispering*) Corned beef?
**Doctor** A sandwich ... a corned beef sandwich.

*Dr Shawcross chews with relish as they scrutinize their sandwiches*

**Mabel** Good gracious ...
**Dorothy** How awful ....

*They see Cressida, smile and bravely eat*

**Aubrey** Did you know if you stab a man in the middle of winter ... steam will rise from the wound?
**Richard** I suppose it would.
**Aubrey** Primitives believed it to be the spirit departing the body.
**Richard** Will you excuse me? (*He moves away*)

# Act I

**Aubrey** But I was just about to ──

*Richard is ambushed by Mabel and Dorothy*

**Mabel** We understand you're the gentleman who poisoned cousin Toby?
**Dorothy** Poisoned poor Toby.
**Richard** Well, I ... I wouldn't quite put it like that.
**Mabel** We hoped you might tell us about the Inquest.
**Dorothy** Oh yes, the Inquest. If it's not ──
**Mabel** If it's not too painful.
**Richard** I'm very sorry ladies, but I'd really rather ──
**Mabel** Young man, we have travelled all the way from Bridlington.
**Dorothy** Bridlington.
**Mabel** A considerable distance.
**Richard** Yes, well ── I hope you have a pleasant journey back. Now if you'll please excuse me, I should like to ──
**Isobel** (*thumping her stick*) Cressida: a word, if you please.

*Cressida obeys*

**Aubrey** But, for me ── for me, you see, it was always a question of psychology ── I assume you're familiar with Freud?
**Doctor** Away with you ── me? You've the wrong man, Inspector. I'm strictly potions and lotions.
**Aubrey** Then you forfeit a whole world of discovery.

*Emily stands beside Richard*

I've spent my entire life probing human nature ──
**Emily** Drinking and smoking, laughing and joking ...
**Aubrey** ── albeit the darker side.
**Richard** Hallo, Emily.
**Emily** It's like a party. I thought we were supposed to be mourning the dead?
**Richard** Each in their own way, Emily. Don't be too ready to judge.
**Emily** They couldn't care a fig. The alcohol was Mama's idea. I think it's shameful. (*She begins to wander off again*)
**Richard** (*following Emily*) Come now ... is it really such a sin? A drop of sherry never ──
**Emily** A drop can lead to an ocean, Mr Harker. And you well know how Papa felt. Mama's making her mark, you see. (*She sits on a step*) Gran's furious. They had a terrible row.
**Richard** (*sitting beside her*) Well, there are bound to be changes, and I'm sure once your mother ──

**Emily** Everything changes. Everything dies. Don't you think that's cruel?
**Richard** It's not cruel, Emily, it's just life. It's the price we pay.
**Emily** Papa died like a dog. Why does God allow such things? All-seeing, all-powerful — yet He does nothing? That seems very cruel to me, Mr Harker.

*Cressida approaches*

**Cressida** Have you tried the chocolate cake? It's delicious. Emily ...?
**Emily** Why were you laughing?
**Cressida** Was I?
**Emily** You were laughing. I saw you. Have you no respect?
**Richard** Now listen here, young lady, that's no way to ——
**Cressida** I'll deal with this, Mr Harker. Darling, what is it? You're being —— (*She moves to touch Emily*)
**Emily** Don't touch me!
**Cressida** I'm only trying to ——
**Emily** (*standing*) Leave me alone! Leave me alone! ... hypocrites!

*All eyes turn to Emily*

(*Pointing accusingly*) Hypocrites! All of you! Sinners! (*She heads for the exit; screaming*) Sinners! Sinners and hypocrites!

*She bolts off*

*Pause*

**Cressida** I'm ... I'm so sorry ...

*Black-out*

*Everyone exits*

*Distant thunder. A pale pool of light slowly rises on Emily, squatting on the library floor, nursing a long-loved rag doll*

**Emily** (*sadly; singing*) Row, row, row the boat
                    Gently down the stream
                    Merrily, merrily, merrily, merrily
                    Life is but a dream

                    Row, row, row the boat
                    Gently down the stream
                    Merrily, merrily ——

Act I                                                                                                11

**Cressida** (*off*) Emily ... Emily ...
**Emily** (*still lost in her private world, echoing tunefully*) Emily, Emily ... merrily, merrily ...
**Cressida** (*closer*) Emily ...
**Emily** (*suddenly looking round, panicking, protectively gripping her doll*) Punished ... I'll be punished ... no, no, please, no — hide, hide ... we must hide. (*She scrambles into the upstage shadows*)

*Cressida enters*

**Cressida** Emily ...?

*More thunder. Cressida comes a little further onstage and suddenly turns*

*Richard enters*

(*Seeing Richard*) Oh, it's you. You gave me such a ——
**Richard** I'm sorry. I didn't mean to startle. (*He pauses*) That was quite an outburst ...
**Cressida** She's upset, she's been very upset. It's perfectly normal.
**Richard** Of course. Of course it is. And what about you? You seem to be coping remarkably well.
**Cressida** Am I? Heaven knows how. I feel as if I'm living a dream. Nothing seems real. I just watch myself do things. It's the strangest feeling.

*In a sudden gush of emotion, Richard holds and comforts Cressida*

**Richard** You'll be fine.
**Cressida** So quickly ... it happened so quickly. I still can't believe it. He's dead. Richard, he's dead. The fat old pig's dead. (*She pauses*) Lock the door.
**Richard** Cressida ...
**Cressida** Lock the door.
**Richard** Not today.
**Cressida** This is the happiest day of my life. Now lock the door. Lock the door.
**Richard** You're incorrigible. (*He locks the door*)

*Cressida kisses Richard*

**Cressida** Love you, love you, love you ...

*Emily edges into the highlight, observing*

**Richard** (*pulling away*) We can't. Cressida, we can't — it's wrong.

**Cressida** That's why it'll be so wonderful ... now love me ... love me, love me ... soothe me ... stroke me ...
**Richard** Cressida ...
**Cressida** (*touching him*) Come into my parlour said the spider to the fly. Well, my darling demon? Will you come? Will you come in my parlour?

*He kisses her and she gently pulls him to the floor*

That's better ... much better ...

*More thunder. A shuddering light reveals Emily, twisting the neck of her rag doll as she watches her mother make love*

*Black-out*

*The storm fades to silence*

*Richard exits*

*The Lights rise upstage on Cressida, methodically brushing Emily's long hair as she sits in her rocking chair*

**Emily** Why did you marry Papa?
**Cressida** (*stopping the brushing momentarily*)What a question.
**Emily** Did you love him?
**Cressida** Darling ——
**Emily** Did you? Did you truly? Did you really truly love him?
**Cressida** Emily, please — I'm very tired.
**Emily** Papa always said the devil was beautiful.
**Cressida** What?
**Emily** The devil, the darling devil.
**Cressida** What on earth are you talking about?
**Emily** The seducer of Eve. He who brings sin and corruption into the world.
**Cressida** That's your father speaking.
**Emily** Father's dead.
**Cressida** What I meant was ——
**Emily** How did he die?
**Cressida** I hardly think ——
**Emily** How, Mother? I know it was food poisoning, but how?

*Pause*

**Cressida** Corned beef. Silly, isn't it? A tin of corned beef. Your father and Mr Harker always shared sandwiches when they went fishing.

# Act I

**Emily** If they shared, why didn't they both die?
**Cressida** I don't know.
**Emily** Don't you think it strange?
**Cressida** Strange? Why strange?
**Emily** I think it's strange.
**Cressida** Don't be silly.
**Emily** I am not silly!
**Cressida** Mr Harker's younger, and ... and healthier and — oh, for heaven's sake — I'm not a doctor. (*She fumbles the hairbrush*) That'll do. Kiss me good-night. Emily ...?
**Emily** (*looking away*) I shall pray for you.
**Cressida** And I ... I shall pray for you.

*The Lights fade to Black*

*Emily and Cressida exit*

*As the Lights fade, Mrs Hodge enters with an oil lamp, aiding Isobel to a downstage chair. Isobel now wears a nightdress and gown*

**Isobel** Thank you, Mrs Hodge.
**Mrs Hodge** Shall I not be helping you to bed?
**Isobel** Let me sit awhile.
**Mrs Hodge** I'll get you some hot milk. A little brandy, maybe.
**Isobel** Brandy?
**Mrs Hodge** Just to help you sleep.
**Isobel** Very well, if you insist. But I shan't sleep tonight.
**Mrs Hodge** Now, now — you mustn't be too hard on her.
**Isobel** Isn't that for me to judge?
**Mrs Hodge** Course, ma'am, certainly. Only it's such a difficult time, isn't it? What with her being, well, you know — half child, half woman. Not that I'm making excuses mind, far from it, but ——
**Isobel** She has disgraced us all. Is it any wonder no decent school will have her?
**Mrs Hodge** Yes, ma'am, only ——
**Isobel** Thank you, Mrs Hodge. You may go.
**Mrs Hodge** (*bobbing*) Yes, ma'am.

*Mrs Hodge leaves. As she does so, Cressida enters*

**Cressida** I've come to say good-night.
**Isobel** Well? Did you beat her? I thought as much.
**Cressida** There's been enough of that.
**Isobel** Spare the rod and spoil the child. Is that what you want?

**Cressida** Please — let's not quarrel.
**Isobel** That outburst was unforgivable. I've never felt so ashamed. Toby must be turning in his grave.
**Cressida** Isobel — she's very distressed.
**Isobel** Distressed? What about me? Am I not distressed? How do you imagine I feel? To bury one's own child is the worst thing in the world. Haven't I suffered enough?
**Cressida** I think we all have.
**Isobel** Yes. Yes, you're right. I have lost a son, but you have not only lost a dear husband but also the father of your child. Forgive me, you must think me very selfish.
**Cressida** There's nothing to forgive.
**Isobel** I do so admire your fortitude.
**Cressida** We each grieve in our own way.

*There is a pause*

I was wondering if next week you might care to play a little bridge?
**Isobel** Bridge?
**Cressida** I suppose it is rather soon. Only I know how much you enjoy it.
**Isobel** Next week, you say?
**Cressida** Or the week after, if you ——
**Isobel** No, no. I'm sure bridge and a cold supper wouldn't be considered too excessive. But no alcohol — on that I insist.
**Cressida** Agreed. I'll invite Aubrey then, shall I?
**Isobel** Provided he doesn't prattle endlessly about his blessed book.
**Cressida** We will of course need a fourth. Isobel ...?
**Isobel** Yes, yes — I'm not deaf. What about Colonel Hutchins?
**Cressida** Yes. Why not? Oh ... I do believe the Colonel's in Town all next week.
**Isobel** Really?
**Cressida** And the week after.
**Isobel** I don't recall him ——
**Cressida** I'm sure he said something. What about Mr Harker?
**Isobel** Harker? Have you lost all sense of propriety? Fishing is one thing, Cressida — bridge is quite another! Heavens above, his people are scarcely better than peasants. Pig-farmers, I believe.
**Cressida** Aren't you being rather stuffy? He did go to university ...
**Isobel** And where's it got him — a common bookseller!
**Cressida** Considering his limited means, he's always perfectly presentable. And more to the point, he plays a fine hand.
**Isobel** Does he indeed? Toby never mentioned.
**Cressida** Toby taught him.

Act I                                                                                                       15

**Isobel** Did he?
**Cressida** Very well, by all accounts. But if you — if you don't think he's suitable ...
**Isobel** I suppose he does have a certain vulgar charm.
**Cressida** I'll ask him then, shall I?
**Isobel** Dr Shawcross; he plays, doesn't he?
**Cressida** No ... I don't think so.
**Isobel** Yes, I'm sure. And I do believe he's rather good.
**Cressida** Oh. Well, if you're certain, if you're absolutely sure. That's — that's settled then. Only ...
**Isobel** Only what?
**Cressida** It's really rather embarrassing. It's just ... well, sometimes — sometimes the way he looks at me ...
**Isobel** What? You mean —
**Cressida** Even today.
**Isobel** Today! Has the man no shame?
**Cressida** Apparently not. I'll ask Mr Harker then, shall I?
**Isobel** Hm?
**Cressida** Mr Harker ...
**Isobel** There's really no-one else, is there? Very well. (*Rising*) Thank you, my dear, most thoughtful. I shall look forward to it. Help me to my bed, would you ... ?

*Cressida picks up the oil-lamp and leads Isobel off*

*The Lights fade to Black-out*

*Aubrey and Emily enter*

**Aubrey** (*from the darkness*) It was indeed murder most foul. Indeed it was at that moment, that very moment, as the true horror gripped my heart, that I knew —

*The Lights now rise on Aubrey, pacing to and fro, reciting histrionically from his manuscript. Emily sits on a stool*

— knew in my bones, indeed in my very soul, that I would never, never rest until this outrageous outrage ... outrageous outrage? Doesn't sound right, does it? Top-notch stuff, though, eh? Rather reminds one of Conrad, don't you think?
**Emily** But why? Why do people murder?
**Aubrey** Good heavens, any number of reasons: greed, revenge ... passion ...
**Emily** Passion?

**Aubrey** It's when, er ... when we allow our emotions to be ruled by ——
**Emily** Desire? Desire of the flesh?
**Aubrey** Exactly.
**Emily** Lust. Adultery. Fornication ...?
**Aubrey** Yes, all that — all that kind of thing.
**Emily** Like animals ... grunting and groaning like beasts of the field.
**Aubrey** We're all animals, Emily. Or so Mr Darwin would have us believe.
**Emily** Papa says Darwin is a Son of Satan.
**Aubrey** That's somewhat strong. Your father always was a man of somewhat extreme ... my dear girl, I'm so sorry. I didn't mean to ——
**Emily** It's not you.
**Aubrey** Then what? What is it, Emily?
**Emily** Everything. The whole world's upside-down and I don't know who to trust any more.
**Aubrey** Can't you even trust me?
**Emily** He might've used a spell ...
**Aubrey** Spell?
**Emily** Mr Harker. He's a beast and a devil, a devil and a demon.
**Aubrey** Now Emily ... haven't we spoken before about ——?
**Emily** It's not a game, it's not. You're a detective, you should know. Isn't it obvious? He's covered with hair and he grunts, he grunts, he grunts like a pig.
**Aubrey** I always thought you liked him.
**Emily** He's wicked — full of sin.
**Aubrey** That's your father speaking.
**Emily** How can he speak if he's dead?
**Aubrey** It's just an expression.
**Emily** Of what? An expression of what?
**Aubrey** Never mind that. I want to know why you suddenly hate Richard? You must surely have a reason?
**Emily** Can't ... can't say ...
**Aubrey** Can't or won't?
**Emily** I knew you wouldn't believe me.
**Aubrey** I don't believe you because I know it's not true.
**Emily** How do you know? How can you possibly?
**Aubrey** I think I know the human character better than most. Richard's a fine fellow, salt of the earth. I'd stake my reputation on it.
**Emily** (*standing*) Thank you for the cocoa.
**Aubrey** Don't you want any cake? I bought it specially.
**Emily** I liked your book.
**Aubrey** You did?
**Emily** It was very interesting.
**Aubrey** Splendid! Tricky stuff this authoring business, I don't mind telling

# Act I                                    17

you. Particularly autobiography. Living one's whole life again. All the good and all the bad. Especially the bad. Dear oh dear, yes, indeed — makes one rather ... what's the word?
**Emily** May I borrow it?
**Aubrey** Hm?
**Emily** Your book?
**Aubrey** Oh. Well, I've only the one copy. But when it's published, I promise you'll be among the first.
**Emily** Then may I borrow another?
**Aubrey** What kind? An adventure, perhaps? Jules Verne?
**Emily** The same as yours. A book about murder. I know you have lots and lots.
**Aubrey** Well yes, but I'm far from certain your mother would approve.
**Emily** Please.
**Aubrey** Unless, of course ——— (*He goes upstage and picks up a distinctive, slim leather-bound volume*) Unless you want the very best? Hm? *La crème de la crème*, so to speak. There you go. I think you'll find this fits the bill. Take it — a little present.
**Emily** (*kissing Aubrey's cheek*) Thank you.
**Aubrey** I'll get your cloak.

*Aubrey exits*

*Emily begins to read and the Lights change as the book begins to cast its spell. Emily becomes progressively captivated, circling her way upstage and finally sitting in her rocking chair. The chair rocks and the sound of a cold wind rises*

**Emily** (*lowering the book and pondering*) A month, a little month? (*She considers this and returns to her book*)

*The Lights begin to change*

*As they do so, Cressida enters. Now free of funereal black, she hums a sweet song, showing off a new evening dress*

**Cressida** Well? Do you like it? Emily ...?
**Emily** A beast that wants discourse of reason would have mourned longer.
**Cressida** What? What did you say?
**Emily** Wormwood ...
**Cressida** Don't you like it?
**Emily** Widow Wormwood.
**Cressida** Emily ...
**Emily** Emily's gone. Emily's dead.

**Cressida** Dead? Whatever do you mean, dead?

*The sound of the cold wind fades*

**Emily** It's because he's coming, isn't it?
**Cressida** Who? Mr Harker?
**Emily** That's why you're so happy.
**Cressida** It'll be nice to see him of course, but he was always your father's friend, not mine. What are you reading? May I see?

*Emily contorts her body, protecting her book*

Emily — I should like to see your book.

*Emily complies*

**Cressida** (*opening the book and smiling*) Ah — Shakespeare ... very good. There now. Was that so terribly difficult? You see — there's no need to be so secretive. (*She returns it*)

*Mrs Hodge enters, bobs*

**Mrs Hodge** Mr Harker, ma'am. I've shown him into the drawing-room.
**Cressida** Thank you.

*Mrs Hodge leaves*

(*Approaching Emily and kneeling*) Aren't you tired of this dress? Why don't you have a change? Something nice and bright? Darling, I know you're still sad, but it makes no sense to stay unhappy. Life's far too short, and much too tragic.
**Emily** Can't you see? You're bewitched. He's put a spell on you.
**Cressida** (*amused*) A spell? Who has?
**Emily** Richard, Richard, Uncle Richard.
**Cressida** You don't miss much, do you?
**Emily** You admit it?
**Cressida** I like him well enough. In fact, I like him very much. I rather thought you did too?
**Emily** Not any more.
**Cressida** You always used to say how handsome he was.
**Emily** The devil hath power to assume a pleasing shape.
**Cressida** What?
**Emily** Mother — God has sent me a sign.

## Act I

**Cressida**  Please ... please don't spoil things.
**Emily**  Repent! You must repent!
**Cressida**  What?
**Emily**  Confess yourself to Heaven, repent what's past, otherwise — otherwise you'll burn in Hell! You'll burn in Hell for all ——
**Cressida**  Stop it!
**Emily**  It's true!
**Cressida**  Stop it!
**Emily**  Your soul is in mortal danger!
**Cressida**  I won't have you spoiling things, I won't.
**Emily**  Pray! You must pray! Mother — pray! Get down on your knees and pray! Pray God will ——

*Cressida slaps Emily's face. Stunned and full of remorse, she then kneels and embraces her daughter*

**Cressida**  I'm sorry ... darling, I'm sorry ...
**Emily**  Please. Mother, please. Pray with me. Please pray with me. God is great. God is merciful.

*Cressida nods in agreement and lowers her head in supplication as Emily leads them in prayer*

**Emily**  } *(together)* { Have mercy on me, O Lord. Wash me thoroughly
**Cressida**                    from my wickedness and cleanse me from my
                                 sin, for I acknowledge my faults ...

*The Lights crossfade to downstage where Richard stands, warming his backside by the fire, which is unseen*

And though our sins be red as scarlet, they shall be made white as snow. And though they be like purple, they shall be made white as wool ...

*Mrs Hodge enters with a bridge table, which she positions on a diagonal*

O Lord, hear our prayer and let our cry come unto thee. Glory be to the Father, and to the Son, and to the Holy Ghost.
**Richard**  Any chance of a drop of Scotch, Mrs Hodge?
**Emily**  Amen.
**Mrs Hodge**  'Fraid not, sir.
**Cressida**  Amen.

*Emily and Cressida exit*

**Mrs Hodge** Lady Isobel doesn't think it proper.
**Richard** Oh ...
**Mrs Hodge** Her ladyship won't be long, sir. She's just seeing Miss Emily to bed. I could get you a cup of tea?
**Richard** No ... no, thank you.
**Mrs Hodge** Glass of hot milk? That'll warm you.
**Richard** Not quite the same, is it?
**Mrs Hodge** I wouldn't know, sir.

*Cressida enters*

**Cressida** (*smiling*) Richard ...
**Richard** (*formally pecking Cressida's cheek*) You look wonderful.
**Cressida** You don't think it's ——?
**Richard** No, no — not at all.

*They stand awkwardly while Mrs Hodge arranges chairs*

**Richard** I seem to be a little early.
**Cressida** No matter. So how are you?
**Richard** Fine. I'm fine. And you?
**Cressida** The same. Much the same. Mrs Hodge ...?
**Mrs Hodge** Yes, ma'am?
**Cressida** There are some fresh playing cards on my dressing-table. Would you kindly fetch them?
**Mrs Hodge** Yes, ma'am ...

*Mrs Hodge leaves*

**Richard** (*urgently making for Cressida*) What's wrong? Something's wrong ...
**Cressida** Nothing.
**Richard** Cressida ...
**Cressida** Emily's being difficult, that's all.
**Richard** Nothing else?
**Cressida** Everything's fine. Relax ...
**Richard** Relax? I've hardly slept a wink. And when I do finally get off, all I dream of is hearts and spades and no trumps and ——
**Cressida** You mean you don't dream of me?
**Richard** No, I damn well don't. I'm glad you find it so amusing. Whatever possessed you? Couldn't you've suggested whist or something? Or — or Newmarket, or ...?
**Cressida** Newmarket? Isobel! The very idea!
**Richard** Oh, it's fine for you — you won't have the old dragon breathing down your ——

Act I                                                                                           21

**Cressida** *Courage, mon brave.*
**Richard** Cressida — you can't learn bridge just from a book.
**Cressida** Yes, you can. You can do anything. Anything. Now shush and let me look at you ... (*She circles her lover*) Oh yes, very elegant ... very — distinguished ... (*She touches him*) Every inch the perfect gentleman. In fact, quite the aristocrat.
**Richard** (*gripping her hand*) Just because I've learned to ape my betters, doesn't mean I approve of them.
**Cressida** (*licking his fingers*) But you — you do approve of me?
**Richard** Does the fly approve of the spider?
**Cressida** My, my — aren't we the clever one? Next time I shall wrap you in my web and gobble you all up ... gobble, gobble, gobble ... bit by bit. Would you like that? Hm? Would you like me to eat you?
**Richard** When?
**Cressida** Soon. Very soon.
**Richard** Tomorrow? Say tomorrow.
**Cressida** No, not tomorrow.
**Richard** Why not?
**Cressida** Too risky.
**Richard** Isn't that what you like? Surely you can ——?

*Isobel approaches, her stick scraping*

*Alerted, the lovers instantly part. Cressida busies herself, precisely positioning score pads. Richard formally greets Isobel*

**Richard** Lady Isobel, how very kind of you to invite me.
**Isobel** (*ignoring Richard, her eyes fixed on Cressida*) Do you really think that dress to be appropriate?
**Cressida** I didn't think it unsuitable, no.
**Isobel** (*picking her way to the table*) It is altogether too colourful.
**Richard** I'm sure Toby wouldn't ——
**Isobel** This does not concern you, Mr Harker.
**Cressida** Would you like me to change?
**Isobel** I should like you to be a little more sensitive. (*She sits*) Mr Harker, in the circumstances you may call me Isobel and I shall call you Richard — is that agreeable?
**Richard** Yes, most — most agreeable.

*Mrs Hodge enters, bobs and announces*

**Mrs Hodge** Chief Inspector Dachett.

*Aubrey enters, rubbing life into his cold hands*

*Mrs Hodge exits*

**Aubrey** Not late, am I? Such a clear night, I thought I'd walk. (*He kisses Cressida*) Cressida, my dear, you look stunning, absolutely stunning.
**Cressida** Thank you, Aubrey.
**Aubrey** (*shaking Richard's hand*) Richard ...
**Richard** You're frozen.
**Aubrey** Yes, damn cold. Begging your pardon, Isobel. (*He kisses her*) So how are you, old girl? Hm? Don't you think Cressida looks a picture?
**Isobel** We don't seem to have any cards.
**Cressida** Mrs Hodge is fetching them.
**Aubrey** I say, you'll never guess what I've just found ... (*He produces the rag doll from a pocket*) Emily's, isn't it? Gertrude, or Charlotte, or something?
**Cressida** Cassandra — her favourite. Where did you find it?
**Aubrey** That's the thing, most peculiar. I was walking by the edge of the forest, thinking about my final chapter — the one I told you about, Richard. The Basingstoke Strangler. Proving to be a bit of a pig, I don't mind telling you ——
**Isobel** Get on with it, man.
**Aubrey** Hm? Oh, yes. Anyway, there I was, musing away, when I noticed something decidedly strange. I know moonlight plays tricks, but it seemed as if it were floating ...
**Cressida** You mean, the doll —— ?
**Aubrey** Yes — floating. Or so it seemed. However, on closer inspection, I discovered it nailed to a tree.
**Isobel** Nailed to a tree?
**Aubrey** Look — you can still see the hole ... (*he pokes a finger into the doll*) Right through the heart.
**Richard** I don't think we need an autopsy, Aubrey.
**Isobel** Quite.
**Aubrey** But don't you think it's, well — odd?
**Isobel** Whatever's the girl playing at?
**Cressida** Oh, I expect it's just another of her games.
**Isobel** Impaling a doll to a tree? What kind of game is that?

*Mrs Hodge enters and places the cards on the table*

**Cressida** Does it really matter?
**Isobel** We shall take supper at nine.
**Mrs Hodge** Yes, ma'am.
**Cressida** (*giving Mrs Hodge the doll*) Mrs Hodge — will you please get rid of this.
**Mrs Hodge** Get rid of it, ma'am?

# Act I

**Cressida** Burn it. I said burn it.
**Mrs Hodge** Very good, ma'am.

*Mrs Hodge leaves*

**Isobel** (*shuffling the cards*) Well then — shall we cut for partners?

*As they do so ...*

*Emily, now wearing a nightdress, enters upstage carrying a candle. She sits in her rocking chair, reads her book*

You and I, Richard. Splendid — Cressida tells me you're something of an expert?
**Richard** Oh, I wouldn't quite ——
**Isobel** Now, now — don't be modest. It flatters a woman, but ill becomes a man. Right then. Shall we get on?

*They take their places at the table*

*As they do so the Lights fade almost to black and the sound of the cold wind slowly rises*

**Emily** (*lowering the book, musing, trance-like*) Remember, remember, must I remember? A father killed, a mother stained? Why, she would hang on him, hang on him ... filthy, dirty — within a month, within a little month ... my father, my poor father ... in the dark, deep in the dark, waiting for the worms.

*The sound of the wind rises and the candle flutters*

Ay, old mole ... canst thou hear me?

*The sound of the wind suddenly fades. Then, from the silence, a man sobs, almost imperceptibly at first, but — electronically amplified — soon rising to fill the theatre with a surreal and profound sadness*

(*Standing and picking up her candle*) Papa? (*She peers into the dark and moves forward*) Papa ...?

*The sobbing stops. Then an invisible power suddenly grips Emily's wrist and forces her to kneel. Despite her resisting, Emily's hand is slowly forced down over the candle flame. She whimpers with pain. The invisible force releases her hand and a voice whispers*

**Voice** That was but a moment. Can you imagine the agony of all eternity?

*Emily slowly nods and the cold wind returns; the sound rises and swells*

    I am thy father's spirit. Revenge. Revenge this most foul and unnatural murder. Revenge. Revenge thy father. (*Fading into the night*) Remember me ... remember me ...

**Emily** (*echoing*) Remember me, remember me ...

*There is laughter from downstage. The candle flickers and blows out. The wind dies. There is more laughter*

*The Lights slowly rise on the bridge table. During the following, Emily appears, standing in her nightdress, lost in another world. Richard sees her*

**Aubrey** ... appearance and reality, quite so — how to tell the good from the bad. You see, they all seemed entirely respectable ——

**Richard** Two hearts.

**Aubrey** — the very epitome of gentility. But I knew — I knew beyond the slightest doubt ——

**Cressida** Two spades.

**Aubrey** — that one of them was a murderer. Yes, sir: a murderer. A mean and squalid soul — cold, ruthless, calculating, capable of any ——

**Isobel** For heaven's sake — do you mind?

**Aubrey** Hm? What?

**Isobel** I am finding your constant preoccupation with murder and all things gruesome extremely distracting. Three hearts.

**Aubrey** You did ask ...

**Isobel** I was merely being polite — I did not anticipate a twenty minute lecture.

**Aubrey** Suppose I do go on. Comes with living on one's own. Only this morning I found myself conversing with the frying pan. Can you imagine? There I was ——

**Isobel** Before you embark on yet another sea of prattle, perhaps we might trouble you for a bid?

**Aubrey** Three spades.

**Isobel** And high time too. Richard? Richard ...?

*Richard is looking at Emily*

**Cressida** (*urgently moving to Emily*) Darling, what is it? (*She kneels and holds Emily*) Tell me ...

**Emily** I've seen Papa. Papa's ghost.

# Act I                                                    25

**Aubrey** Ghost?
**Isobel** What? What did she say?
**Emily** My father's spirit.
**Isobel** (*crossing herself*) God in Heaven!
**Cressida** (*glaring at Isobel, then comforting Emily*) Poor darling ... it was a dream, only a ——
**Emily** It was real.
**Cressida** No, darling, it was ——
**Emily** It was real. It was Papa. He was crying.
**Isobel** Crying?
**Cressida** Isobel, please.
**Emily** Crying and crying.
**Isobel** You mean Toby, you mean your father, your father was ——
**Cressida** Isobel! Emily, if this is another of your ——
**Isobel** My poor boy ... my poor, dear boy ...
**Cressida** She's had a dream! A bad dream!
**Isobel** How do you know? How can you be so certain? I tell you, there are more things in heaven ——
**Cressida** Oh, shut up, you stupid woman! Can't you see? You're making her worse!
**Isobel** (*rising*) How dare you!
**Richard** Cressida ...
**Cressida** I'm ... I'm sorry.
**Isobel** Never in all my days ...
**Aubrey** Steady on, old girl. We're all a bit ——
**Isobel** How dare she speak to me like that! I'll not have it, Aubrey, I won't!
**Emily** Papa wants revenge.
**Aubrey** Revenge?
**Emily** That's why his ghost came back.
**Richard** You mean — you mean he spoke?
**Cressida** Richard! For God's sake!
**Emily** (*confronting Richard, eyes wild*) He said you were a serpent, a stinging serpent. He said you were horrible — horrible, horrible, most horrible.
**Cressida** Emily!
**Emily** And that soon — soon you'll burn in Hell!

*Richard turns away, devastated*

**Aubrey** (*approaching Emily*) You mustn't say such dreadful things. There are no such things as ghosts and I'll hear no more of these ridiculous fantasies. And I certainly won't have you blaming Richard. What happened was an accident. Yes, Emily — an accident. Don't you think the poor fellow's suffered enough?

**Richard** Your father was my friend — I wouldn't hurt him for the world.
**Emily** Liar!
**Cressida** Emily!
**Emily** Lies! Lies! All lies! See how the villain smiles!
**Cressida** Emily Arlington — you will go to bed at once!
**Emily** Don't touch me! Whore! Filthy whore! Filthy, dirty — that's why, that's why he was crying! That's why he ——
**Isobel** (*smashing down her stick across the table*)Silence! Not another word! (*She approaches Emily, pointing her stick*) Not another word! Or God help me I'll beat this madness out of you!
**Emily** Better mad with truth than sane with lies.
**Isobel** (*raising her stick*) Wicked, wicked girl!
**Cressida** (*shielding Emily*) Don't you dare!
**Isobel** (*pointing her stick*) I warn you — one more word and I shall have you sent to the asylum!

*Terrified, Emily covers her mouth*

**Cressida** (*holding Emily tight*) Don't say that! Don't ever say that!

*Confrontation*

**Isobel** (*backing down and turning away*) Get her out of my sight.

*Aubrey helps Isobel to a chair*

**Cressida** Go to your room. You will go to your room and stay there a week. A whole week, do you understand? Answer me!

*There is no response. Emily's crossed hands still cover her mouth*

Answer me!
**Isobel** You see — stubborn. Stubborn and stupid.
**Aubrey** Go to bed, Emily.

*Emily glares at Richard, then leaves*

*There is a long pause*

**Isobel** We must face the facts — the child is depraved.
**Cressida** The child is grieving! Can't you understand? All she needs is a little time, a little love and kindness, but all she ever gets from you ——
**Richard** Cressida ——

Act I 27

**Isobel** A whore! She called you a whore! Is that normal? Is that sane? Well? Is it?
**Aubrey** As normal as sex and death. Primeval forces, Isobel. And a uniquely powerful combination. I suppose Freud would ——
**Isobel** Freud be damned! Her own mother, Aubrey: have you ever heard the like? And where does she learn such language? Hm? The village boys, no doubt. Oh yes, oh yes. I tell you, the sooner she's married off the better. Always assuming we can find someone fool enough to have her.

*There is a pause*

**Cressida** I think I'll take a breath of air. Anyone care to join me?

*Black-out*

*Everyone exits. The bridge table is removed*

*Moonlight. A peacock screams in the night*

*Richard enters, followed by Cressida*

**Cressida** (*whispering intensely*) Will you get a grip? Richard ...!
**Richard** Is it possible? Can it be possible that somehow ... somehow his spirit ——
**Cressida** Don't be ridiculous! It was a dream, only a ——
**Richard** But her eyes ——
**Cressida** She's always had a vivid imagination.
**Richard** Cressida, her eyes, the way she looked at me — I swear it was as if she knew.
**Cressida** Her mind is full of fancy. It's a game. She makes everything a game.
**Richard** Game or not, how can it explain —— ?
**Cressida** What are you saying?
**Richard** I tell you, she knows! And if it's not a ghost, how could she possibly know from a dream?
**Cressida** Stop it!
**Richard** Revenge. Whatever it is, that's what it said. Revenge. Now what the hell does ——?
**Cressida** Stop it! Stop it! What are you trying to do? Have you lost all reason? I have to live in that house!
**Richard** No you don't! Leave! Leave the damn place!
**Cressida** And do what? Take in washing?
**Richard** We'll manage.

**Cressida** Manage? I am Lady Arlington!
**Richard** And I'm nothing, is that it?
**Cressida** I love you!
**Richard** Then marry me. (*He pauses*) I see. Good enough to eat, but not to wed?
**Cressida** Don't be crude.
**Richard** Pardon me for being so bold. I shall endeavour to remember my place.
**Cressida** You don't know what you're asking ——
**Richard** Don't I? So who's next? Some rich old baron, perhaps? Another fat and fancy title?
**Cressida** How little you know me.
**Richard** Well enough, my lady, well enough.
**Cressida** I've risked everything for you, you know I'd do anything ——
**Richard** Then marry me. Marry me.

*There is a pause*

**Cressida** Is that really what you want?
**Richard** You will?
**Cressida** If it's what you want ...
**Richard** (*smiling and holding Cressida*) I swear I won't let you down.
**Cressida** Forever and ever?
**Richard** Forever and ever ...

*They kiss*

*Clouds black out the moon and a giant shadow smothers the lovers*

*The sound of the deep and laboured breathing of a dying man fades up. The breathing becomes progressively more erratic*

*Cressida opens her eyes and stares at Richard. Horrified, she slowly recoils*

What's wrong? Cressida ...?

*The moon escapes the clouds and the sound of breathing fades to silence*

   What is it?

*Cressida eventually finds the courage to look at Richard*

   Why did you —— ?

*Her trembling hand explores his face*

   Cressida ... what is it?

# Act I

**Cressida** Nothing ...
**Richard** Nothing? You're shaking.
**Cressida** We'd better be getting back.
**Richard** (*holding Cressida*) A few minutes. A few more ——
**Cressida** (*pulling away*) I want to go back!
**Richard** Cressida ...

*She leaves*

*Deep in the dead of night, a peacock screams. Startled, Richard looks round*

*Black-out*

*Richard exits*

*The Lights rise on Emily, sitting in her rocking chair, reading her book*

*Dr Shawcross, carrying a Gladstone bag, enters with Cressida. They observe a moment, then Dr Shawcross approaches and kneels before Emily*

**Doctor** Hallo, Emily ...

*No response*

Emily — do you know who I am?

*She looks up and nods*

And who am I? Hm? Tell me. Tell me who I am.

*She grins and pretends to take off her socks and shoes*

*Cressida and Dr Shawcross exchange a look of concern*

*Emily stands. In a stylized action, she raises her hand and scans an imaginary horizon, then skips downstage, where she raises her skirts and seems to dance a little jig, suddenly lifting her arms in mock-horror, before skipping backwards in quick retreat*

*Cressida laughs. Dr Shawcross remains nonplussed*

**Cressida** Shore ... sea-shore ...
**Doctor** (*laughing*) Of course!

*Emily makes the sign of the cross*

And a cross — Shore-Cross.

*Emily nods and mimes a stethoscope*

> Dr Shore-Cross ... My, my ... what a clever girl you are. And might you be knowing who the King of England is?

*Emily runs her hands over her face and hair*

**Cressida** (*chuckling*) Oh, that's easy.
**Doctor** (*peremptorily raising his hand*) No, no — please ... let me.

*Emily tries to remove her head*

> Ah, yes ... I see — head!

*Emily nods, then indicates her book, frantically flicking the pages*

> Shakespeare? You think Shakespeare is the king of ——

*Emily shakes her head, pointing insistently*

> No? What then? (*Looking closer at the book and reading*) "The undiscovered country from ..." — no? Well then, I'm flummoxed, haven't a clue. Why don't you just tell me, hm?

*Emily flicks through her book again, rapidly running a finger along the verse*

> Lines? Head-lines?

*Emily stops, exasperated*

> (*Acknowledging defeat*) Words, words, words. That's what you mean, isn't it?

*Emily nods and contracts her hands*

> Ay, I know ... not words — *word*. Head-word.

*Emily nods and smiles*

> Head-word, indeed!

*Emily counts on her fingers*

> Four, five, six ... seven. (*Chuckling and turning to Cressida*) Head-Word the Seventh!

# Act I

**Cressida** (*fondly*) She's always loved games.
**Doctor** Ay, I know and that's all very fine and good, but what kind of game is this? You have your poor mother worried sick. Don't you think it's gone on long enough?

*No response*

> Emily — why won't you speak to me?

*Emily retreats to her rocking chair and her book*

> Maybe if I had a wee word with her on my own?

**Cressida** If you ... if you really think it necessary.
**Doctor** It might help.
**Cressida** (*leaving*) Very well ... I shall be in the conservatory.

*She exits*

**Doctor** Now will you talk to me?

*No response*

> How am I to help if you won't talk? Emily, I'm a simple country doctor, I have no magic wand. But if you'll trust me, whatever it is, I promise I'll try and help. Now will you do that? Hm?

*Emily begins to rock in her chair*

> You can't keep it all bottled up. That's not healthy, not at all. It weakens the mind and troubles the soul. You can make yourself very ill.

*She rocks the chair faster*

> Emily — how long have I know you? Surely you can trust me?

*Faster and faster*

> Come on now — tell me. Tell me what it is ...

*Dr Shawcross stands, sighs and leaves*

*The Lights fade to a pool around Emily and the sound of the cold wind rises*

*The chair rocks violently as Emily grips her head, shaking from side to side, deeply distressed*

**Emily** (*muttering*) Go away ... go away ... go away ...

*The sound of the wind fades away. Then — as if from another world — we faintly hear a beautiful waltz, "The Emperor Waltz." Emily's rocking slows to a stop. She stands and — as if in a dream — sways rhythmically before following the music and dancing her way downstage*

*The Lights change and "The Emperor Waltz" suddenly swells*

*Richard and Cressida sweep on stage in high Prussian style and waltz round and around Emily. She stands transfixed, mesmerized*

*Two other waltzing couples join in — Dorothy and Aubrey, Mabel and Dr Shawcross*

*Mrs Hodge helps Isobel to a downstage chair, where she sits resting on her stick, her demeanour sour and disapproving*

*The waltz ends to polite applause. As this happens:*

*The Rector enters and observes benignly*

**Richard** (*raising his hands, requesting silence*) Ladies and gentlemen, your indulgence please. Cressida — Cressida and I would like to share a secret with you ...

*Reactions*

The truth — the simple truth is that we have fallen in love. And I'm ——

*More reactions*

— I'm delighted to tell you, Cressida — dear, darling Cressida — has done me the honour of consenting to become my wife.
**Aubrey** Bravo! Well done old man!
**Mabel** My dear! What a surprise!
**Dorothy** Such a surprise!
**Mrs Hodge** Oh, ma'am — that's marvellous!
**Rector** Yes, marvellous! Absolutely marvellous!
**Mabel** Isn't she a dark horse?
**Doctor** She is that. All the best, Cressida.

Act I                                                                33

**Dorothy**  Oh yes, all the best!
**Doctor**  And you, Richard, you lucky devil!
**Emily**  Devil?
**Rector**  Now, now, Dr Shawcross ——
**Emily**  Devil?
**Rector**  — do I detect a tiny twinge of envy?

*Laughter*

**Emily**  They know — they all know.
**Rector**  And when shall I have the honour of officiating?
**Emily**  They know and they do nothing.

*More laughter. Richard slides an engagement ring on to Cressida's finger and there are happy sighs from the others*

**Richard**  Love you ——
**Cressida**  Forever and ever?
**Richard**  Forever and ever.

*They kiss*

**Aubrey** (*singing*)     For they are jolly good ——

*The group joins in*

**Group**                      — fellows
           For they are jolly good fellows
           For they are jolly good fell — ows
           Which nobody can deny.

*Emily recoils downstage, covering her ears, closing out the world. But Cressida has eyes only for Richard*

                 Which nobody can deny
                 Which nobody can deny
                 For they are jolly good fell — ows
                 Which nobody can ——

*Emily's distress increases, the singing "loops" surreally*

     — which nobody can, which nobody can ... nobody can, nobody can ——

*Seeing her distress, Aubrey approaches Emily and kneels*

— nobody can ... nobody, nobody ... nobody, nobody ... nobody can, nobody can ——

*Emily gently lowers her hands*

— nobody can deny!

*More cheers and applause*

**Aubrey** Now, now: you'll see. Mark my words — he'll make your mother very happy. And he'll make you a fine father, if only you'd give him half a chance.

*Emily wiggles two fingers, indicating devilish horns*

Won't you even try? Whatever it is, can't you forgive him? Isn't that what God would ——?

*Isobel pounds her stick. There is silence*

**Isobel** (*rising imperiously*) And why was I not consulted?
**Richard** Lady Isobel, we did hope that you might ——
**Isobel** Why was I not consulted?
**Cressida** Because we didn't imagine for one moment you'd agree.
**Richard** Try and understand. We're in love. We're in love and we want to be ——
**Isobel** Mr Harker, you presume too much. Your affection is not at issue. My concern is your suitability. I should have known you had ambitions far above your station. Well it won't do, sir. It won't do at all.
**Richard** I'm not ashamed of what I am. Or what I've been.
**Isobel** No offence, Mr Harker. It is simply a question of quality.
**Aubrey** Isobel, I really do think ——
**Isobel** Don't you "Isobel" me. I detect your hand in this, Aubrey, and don't you deny it. You have long been a valued friend of this family but that does not give you the right to meddle. Yes, Aubrey — meddle. It's as clear as day. And as for you pair of bleating ninnies: have you lost leave of your senses? How dare you applaud this travesty!
**Mabel** Travesty? Whatever do you mean? We naturally assumed Mr Harker ——
**Isobel** Harker has neither money nor position.
**Mabel** Oh.
**Dorothy** Oh, dear ...
**Isobel** His people are pig-farmers.

Act I                                                                                   35

**Mabel** Oh.
**Dorothy** Oh, dear ...
**Isobel** Precisely. He insinuates himself into the very bosom of our family and you howl your thanks like the mob at the foot of the guillotine! Yes, Dorothy — the guillotine. You may well tremble. Who knows where it might end. Have you no sense of history? At all costs, we must maintain standards. (*She returns to her chair*) There will be no wedding. I forbid it. (*She sits*)
**Cressida** (*approaching*) Have you quite finished?
**Isobel** I shall speak to you later.
**Cressida** You'll speak to me now.
**Richard** Cressida ...
**Cressida** No, Richard — how dare she! Sixteen years I've lived in this house. Sixteen years of fear and misery. Sixteen years living under the shadow of you and your foul son ——
**Isobel** Foul son!
**Cressida** And now I've had enough.
**Isobel** You don't know what you're saying ——
**Cressida** I want to live. I want to live my own life.
**Isobel** God forgive you!
**Cressida** Richard is good and kind and I love him. And soon, very soon I shall marry him. And nothing. Nothing will stop me. There. There I've said it.

*The guests are astonished*

(*Returning to the guests*) I do apologize. Should any of you feel disgraced by our happiness, I suggest you leave now. If, however, you would like to be our guests for turkey and Christmas pudding, you will be most welcome. (*She offers her arm to Richard*) Richard ...

*Richard leads Cressida off*

*Mrs Hodge exits*

*The guests stand uncertainly, chattering in hushed whispers. Dr Shawcross approaches Mabel and Dorothy*

**Doctor** Now then — which of you two bonnie young lassies am I to take to dinner?
**Mabel** Dr Shawcross — you ought to be ashamed!
**Dorothy** Ashamed!
**Doctor** Not at all. You're as young as you feel. Now isn't that right?

**Mabel** Oh, yes — yes, indeed.
**Dorothy** Absolutely.
**Mabel** But, well, I — I really don't know. I mean ——
**Doctor** Away with you! And here's me taking you for a romantic ——
**Mabel** You did? You do? Well naturally one feels a certain empathy ...
**Doctor** Of course you do. Come now — it's Christmas.
**Dorothy** Yes, Mabel: Christmas.
**Doctor** Don't you agree, Rector?
**Rector** Indeed so, Doctor: *Amor Vincit Omnia.*
**Mabel** I beg your pardon?
**Doctor** It's Latin: "Love conquers all."
**Mabel** Ah yes. Charming ...
**Dorothy** Delightful.
**Doctor** Shall we ...? (*He offers his arm*)
**Mabel** (*conceding, accepting Dr Shawcross's arm*) Well, if you ... if you really think ——
**Doctor** Oh, I do, I do.

*Dorothy copies Mabel and accompanies the Rector. As they pass Emily, she recoils into the shadows*

**Mabel** (*whispering*) What exactly's wrong with her?

*The two couples head for the exit*

**Doctor** I only wish I knew.

*They exit*

**Aubrey** (*approaching Isobel*) Is it really such a calamity?
**Isobel** Go away.
**Aubrey** Is it?
**Isobel** I said go away.
**Aubrey** Are you going to be sensible about this?
**Isobel** A common bookseller when she could have the pick of the county and you ask me to be sensible?
**Aubrey** Isobel, they're in love ...
**Isobel** For pity's sake, Aubrey — the son of a pig-farmer! One must have some standards.
**Aubrey** He's a decent enough fellow, educated, been to university, it's not as if ——
**Isobel** The man's an upstart, and there's an end of it. But as for her ... as for her — God in Heaven, how could she say such things? Such dreadful, dreadful things.
**Aubrey** She was upset. We all say things ——

Act I                                          37

**Isobel** She humiliated me.
**Aubrey** No more than you did her.
**Isobel** If only she'd given him a son ... Poor Toby. Scarcely a year, scarcely a year and all but forgotten.
**Aubrey** They were never happy, and well you know it.
**Isobel** Happy or not, he made her a lady. Moulded her into a woman of character and distinction. Or so I thought.
**Aubrey** Too much religion, too little love. That's the top and the bottom — you've only got to look at Emily ——
**Isobel** Are you suggesting ——?
**Aubrey** I'm suggesting she needs a father. Yes, Isobel. And I'm also suggesting you let a little light into your life before it's too late.
**Isobel** Don't be impertinent! What's happening with the world? It's all coming to an end. No sense of decency, propriety. It's been one torment after another. Sometimes I fear God has cursed us ...
**Aubrey** You Arlingtons — you curse yourselves. Damn it, woman — if he makes her happy, what else matters? At least give them a chance. Now, come on, up you get. Let me take you to dinner, hm?
**Isobel** I'd sooner starve.
**Aubrey** (*storming towards the exit*) Sometimes ... sometimes you make me so angry!

*He exits*

*Isobel sits alone, contrite*

**Isobel** (*sighing*) Oh dear ...

*Emily appears from the shadows*

Oh, it's you, is it? Been spying, have you? Hm? Up to your old tricks again, eh? Mind you, dumb as you are, you were certainly right about him. He is a demon, isn't he? And an upstart. Probably a scoundrel if only your stupid mother could ——
**Emily** Listen ——
**Isobel** Oh ... finally decided to speak, have we? Well let me tell you, young lady ——
**Emily** Listen. This time listen ... (*She glances round, whispers into Isobel's ear*)
**Isobel** What's that? What? What did you ——? Funeral?
**Emily** The funeral. The day of my father's funeral ... (*She whispers again*)
**Isobel** They did what!!?

*More whispering*

The library? In the library!

**Emily** Now do you see? Now do you understand?

*Mrs Hodge enters*

**Mrs Hodge** Miss Emily, her ladyship says you're to come right away.

*Mrs Hodge leads Emily firmly away during the following*

Come along now — there's been quite enough upset for one day.

*Mrs Hodge and Emily exit*

*The Lights fade until Isobel becomes a featureless silhouette*

**Isobel** (*murmuring*) The library? In the library? How could they? How could they?

*From the dark, we hear the group approaching singing*

**Group** (*off; singing*) Silent night, Holy night
All is calm, all is bright

*The group enters. Lit only by candles, they snake their way downstage where they gather round Isobel*

Round yon Virgin, Mother and Child
Holy Infant so tender and mild

*Isobel struggles to her feet and approaches Richard and Cressida*

Sleep in Heavenly peace
Sleep in Heavenly ——

*Isobel stumbles and the singing falters*

**Aubrey** (*moving to Isobel*) What is it, old girl?

*Isobel gestures Aubrey away, shivering with fury. Barely able to support herself, she nevertheless manages to confront Cressida*

**Isobel** How could you?
**Cressida** Isobel?
**Isobel** Disgusting ...
**Cressida** *Silent Night* — it's your favourite.

Act I                                                                39

**Isobel**  It's the most disgusting — most vile, wicked ——
**Cressida**  I thought you'd be pleased.
**Isobel**  Pleased? You thought ... you thought I'd be —— (*Regaining her strength, she turns on Richard*) And as for you ... as for you ...

*The sound of the cold wind rises. Isobel and Richard stare at one another. Isobel suddenly struggles for breath — a series of convulsions jerk her body. Mabel and Dorothy scream. Richard stands frozen with horror as Isobel crumples in front of him*

**Aubrey**  (*rushing to support Isobel*) Isobel!
**Doctor**  (*pushing through*) Excuse me!
**Mabel**  Oh, my dear! Oh, my dear!
**Doctor**  Out the way — will you please mind out the way!

*Dr Shawcross helps Aubrey lower her to the floor, where he makes a cursory examination*

Hold her head, support her head.
**Mabel**  Oh my dear, my dear ...
**Dorothy**  What's happening, what's happening?
**Rector**  Gentlemen, if I can be of any ——
**Doctor**  All of you — please keep back!
**Aubrey**  You're all right, you're all right.

*Emily approaches, staring down at her dying grandmother*

Don't worry, old girl. I'll look after you. You'll be fine.

*Emily stares at Richard*

**Cressida**  (*approaching and kneeling by Isobel*) Doctor — what is it?

*They all freeze into a tableau — except for Emily*

**Emily**  Too powerful. He's too powerful. His evil eye casts its spell and she withers like a straw. A straw. There is quarrel in a straw. Death and danger dare even for a straw when honour is at the stake ... the stake, at the stake. They burn, burn women, they burn women at the stake. Evil women, wicked woman, sinful women. They hear voices and they burn them, they burn them and send them to Hell.
**Voice**  That was but a moment. Can you imagine the agony of all eternity?
**Emily**  I am dead, sick at heart, forbid to tell the secrets of my prison house. A father killed, a mother stained, and now — now this croaking raven doth bellow for revenge.

**Voice** Revenge. Revenge thy Father.
**Emily** The churchyard yawns and Hell itself breathes out!

*Emily breathes out her candle and vanishes*

**Cressida** Doctor, what is it?
**Doctor** A stroke. It's a stroke. And a bad one.
**Richard** Will she — will she live?
**Doctor** I very much doubt it.

*Cressida enters Richard's embrace*

**Cressida** Tonight? Why tonight?

*The sound of the cold wind swells and the candles flicker, casting strange shadows before being suddenly extinguished*

# ACT II

*The sound of a cold wind blowing can be heard*

*A pool of Light slowly rises on Emily sitting on a step, her long hair woven with flowers, pretty as a picture in her bridesmaid's dress. She is holding her book. She looks up and stares out*

**Emily** How all occasions do inform against me and spur my dull revenge. (*She grips her book, stands and moves downstage*) If it be now, 'tis not to come. If it be not to come, it will be now. If it be not now, yet it will come, in the night, in the night, in the dead vast middle of the night. The readiness is all.

*The sound of the cold wind dies and the Lights slowly fill the stage*

*Aubrey can be heard approaching, "pom-pomming" the "Bridal March", off*

   *Aubrey enters wearing a morning suit, pushing the wheelchair that now imprisons Isobel*

**Aubrey** There we are, old girl.

*She moans, barely audible*

   Hm? Ah, yes. Yes, I see ... (*Adjusting her travel-rug*) There. That's better, isn't it? (*He turns to Emily and smiles*) Won't be long now, eh? How's your mother getting on? Expect it's chaos up there, hm? Don't suppose she looks half as pretty as you, mind. Best let that be our little secret, though — don't want to upset her, do we? Not today. You'll see — once this is over, things'll soon get better.

*Emily nods*

   There we are — better already. Certainly hope so. Truth to tell, my day started rather badly. My book. My poor book. Another rejection. Yes. 'Fraid so. Bit of a disappointment. Not just the book, you see. It's ... well, it's me — what I was, what I achieved. But no-one seems interested. Hey-ho ...

*Emily hugs Aubrey*

Oh, I say. I am privileged. You are a darling girl. Thank you. (*He kneels*) Emily, listen. A few words from you, and you'd make this the happiest day of their lives. It's true. You would. Oh, Emily ... pride, stubborn, foolish pride. Well, if you won't do it for them, will you do it for me? Please. A few words. A few words, that's all.

*Mabel and Dorothy enter from upstage, dressed in their finest*

**Mabel** Well? Will we do?
**Dorothy** Will we? Will we do?
**Aubrey** Do?
**Mabel** Do.
**Aubrey** Ah — do. Yes. Yes, indeed. Splendid. And you Dorothy. Wonderful colours, both of you. Quite exotic. You rather remind me of a pair of parrots.
**Mabel** Parrots!
**Dorothy** Parrots?
**Aubrey** I mean it entirely as a compliment. Splash of colour, just what the occasion needs. And what about Emily, eh? Don't you think she looks a proper lady?
**Mabel** She does indeed — most fetching.
**Dorothy** Oh yes. Doesn't she look pretty?
**Mabel** Terribly feminine. And I do so like the flowers.
**Dorothy** Oh yes, the flowers. The flowers are particularly ——
**Mabel** I expect it won't be too long before you're walking up the aisle yourself, my dear?

*Emily draws a finger across her throat*

What? Don't want to be a bride? Don't be silly, of course you do. It's every girl's dream. Isn't that so, Dorothy?
**Dorothy** Oh yes.
**Mabel** Mind you, it might help if you smiled a little. Doesn't she say anything at all?
**Aubrey** 'Fraid not.
**Mabel** Well it's certainly not from ourside of the family. Which reminds me. How is the bride? Has she been seen?
**Aubrey** Not yet. Dear oh dear, look at the time! Hadn't you better make tracks?
**Mabel** Don't fuss, Aubrey. We're taking the motor car, won't take a minute. Isobel seems a little more perky this morning.

# Act II

**Dorothy** Oh yes ... I do believe she is.
**Mabel** I expect it's all the excitement.
**Dorothy** What a peculiar hat.
**Mabel** It is rather.
**Aubrey** Cressida chose it.
**Mabel** Did she now?

*Isobel struggles to speak*

*Emily slips away, unnoticed*

We were saying how much we like your hat. Your hat. Yes. Most unusual. Is she all ready, Aubrey?
**Aubrey** Ready as she'll ever be.
**Mabel** I mean has she been?
**Aubrey** Been?
**Mabel** Isobel — have you been?
**Aubrey** Oh, I'm sure, Mrs Hodge will have ——
**Mabel** Don't want any accidents, do we? And do try and cheer up. Like it or lump it, we must move with the times.
**Dorothy** Yes we must, like it or lump it.
**Mabel** Mind you ... I trust we shan't be having cold pork at the reception? As you well know, some of the family can be dreadful snobs. Best not fuel their fire, especially Uncle George.

*Isobel moans*

Yes, I know. You never did get on, did you?

*Mrs Hodge — wearing her Sunday best — rushes on*

**Mrs Hodge** Ever so sorry, sir. Forgot my gloves. Won't be a minute ... (*She hurries up the steps*)

*Cressida, radiant in her bridal dress, carrying a posy of wild flowers, enters at the top of the steps. She meets Mrs Hodge*

Oh, ma'am, you look, you look just — just ——
**Cressida** Thank you, Mrs Hodge.
**Mrs Hodge** May I wish you and Mr Richard ——
**Cressida** Why aren't you at the church? You should be at the church.
**Mrs Hodge** I was just fetching my gloves, ma'am.
**Cressida** Well get along then.

**Mrs Hodge**  Yes, ma'am. Sorry, ma'am.
**Cressida**  And be quick.

*Mrs Hodge exits*

*Cressida poses on the steps, smiling*

**Aubrey**  My dear Cressida — you look wonderful, absolutely wonderful.
**Mabel**  Doesn't she, Dorothy?
**Dorothy**  Like a princess.
**Aubrey**  Absolutely.

*Isobel moans as she strains to turn her head, her clawed hand beating the arm-rest*

Goodness me. I'm so sorry, old girl. (*He turns the wheelchair to face Cressida*) There we are. Isn't she perfect?

*Isobel moans her hate. Cressida's smile abruptly sours. She quickly composes herself, descends the steps, and displays her dress. Isobel moans more*

**Cressida**  Oh dear. Don't you like it, Isobel? What's wrong? A little too flamboyant, perhaps? Hm? Or is it the colour?
**Aubrey**  Cressida ——
**Cressida**  What did you have in mind? Scarlet, perhaps?
**Aubrey**  Hasn't she suffered enough?
**Cressida**  No more than she deserves.
**Aubrey**  That's a dreadful thing to say.
**Cressida**  What ye sow ye shall reap. It's how I feel. It's how she's made me feel. This is what happens when people live without love. They end up destroying each other. Why do you think Emily's the way she is? Where is she?
**Aubrey**  Where the devil —— ? She was here a moment ago.
**Cressida**  (*moving to the foot of the steps and calling*) Emily! Emily!

*Mrs Hodge enters, pulling on her gloves*

Mrs Hodge, have you seen Emily?
**Mrs Hodge**  No, ma'am. Not since breakfast. Do you want me to —— ?
**Cressida**  No, no — you're late enough already.
**Mabel**  Perhaps we could take Isobel?
**Dorothy**  Yes, why don't we take her?

# Act II 45

**Mabel** Won't take a minute in the motor car.
**Dorothy** Not in the motor car.
**Cressida** Would you mind?
**Mabel** Consider it done.
**Dorothy** Of course we don't mind, we're delighted to ——
**Mabel** Dorothy! The wheelchair! No time to gabble!

*Dorothy obeys*

Don't worry, my dear. I'm sure she'll turn up. A touch of the collywobbles, I expect. Are we all set then? There — you see? No trouble at all. Come along, Dorothy.

*They exit, Mabel leading the way, Dorothy following pushing Isobel*

**Cressida** Search the house ...
**Mrs Hodge** What about the woods and the garden, ma'am? Shall I get Mr Hargreaves to —— ?
**Cressida** Yes, yes. Everyone. Get everyone.
**Mrs Hodge** *(moving to leave)* Very good, ma'am.
**Cressida** How can she do this? How can she do this?
**Aubrey** Don't get yourself all worked up. Besides, it might well be for the best ...
**Cressida** The best? Yes. Yes, you could be right. The sooner we get this over with —— *(Another flush of anxiety)*
**Aubrey** *(holding Cressida)* Now, now ...
**Cressida** I'm making a perfect fool of myself.
**Aubrey** You'll be fine ... everything'll be fine.
**Cressida** Of course it will. *(Kissing Aubrey's cheek)* You've been so kind.
**Aubrey** All I want is for you to be happy. Heaven knows, you deserve it.
**Cressida** Oh, I'll be happy. I love him so much.
**Aubrey** He's a fine fellow. And a damned lucky one. Well then — shall I escort my princess to her prince?

*Cressida smiles and takes Aubrey's arm. He proudly leads her off*

*As they go, the Lights fade. From the black, we hear a church organ playing Bach's "Jesu, Joy of Man's Desiring". A tight spot slowly rises on a golden cross suspended by thin wire so that it looks as if it is floating. Beneath, the Lights rise on the Rector in conversation with Richard and Dr Shawcross. Two small cushioned stools sit c and a set of steps leads from mid-apron to the auditorium. The theatre is now a church, the audience a congregation*

*Mabel bustles into the auditorium and marches down the aisle, followed by Dorothy pushing Isobel*

**Mabel** (*picking out a member of the audience*) Excuse me ... You, sir! Yes, you! Are you bride or are you groom?

*Dr Shawcross approaches up the aisle and whispers to Dorothy*

Well? Are you gone deaf? Are you bride or groom?
**Dorothy** Mabel — I do believe we're over there ...
**Mabel** Hm? Ah yes, I see — there's Uncle George. Oh, Dr Shawcross ... (*she hurries after him*) Dr Shawcross — a word if I may!
**Dorothy** (*remaining and addressing the member of the audience*) We've come all the way from Bridlington, don't you know? A considerable distance. Oh yes. I understand your family keep pigs? Oh. Goodness me, I'm so sorry. We're not supposed to mention pigs, are we?
**Mabel** Dorothy!
**Dorothy** Perhaps we might meet later?
**Mabel** Dorothy!
**Dorothy** Must dash. (*She wheels Isobel to the foot of the stage*)

*Richard looks at his pocket-watch. Dr Shawcross smiles reassuringly. Prompted by the Rector, the Bach abruptly concludes. The Rector formally steps forward, adjusts his cassock, and adopts a priestly pose. He then smiles, gestures and addresses the audience*

**Rector** Will you all please stand ...

*The organ — still in urgent need of restoration — wheezes before striking up the "Wedding March"*

*After a few bars, Mrs Hodge enters and scuttles down the aisle. She then bobs and crosses herself*

*The music dies ignominiously*

**Mrs Hodge** Every so sorry, Rector. They're just coming up behind. (*She escapes to the nearest seat*)

*The "Wedding March" strikes up again and this time Aubrey escorts the bride through the auditorium, up the steps and on to the stage*

*The Rector gestures for the audience to sit. Isobel moans*

Act II                                                                                          47

**Rector** (*ignoring Isobel; with a smile*) Dearly Beloved, we are gathered together in the sight of God and in the face of this Congregation to join together ——
**Isobel** — forn — forn ——
**Rector**  — to join together this man and this woman in holy Matrimony, which is ——
**Isobel** — forn — forn — forn ——
**Rector** — which is an honourable estate, and is therefore not to be taken in hand ——
**Isobel** — forn — forn — ni — cate — fornicate ——
**Rector**  — in hand unadvisedly, lightly, or wantonly to satisfy men's carnal ——
**Isobel** — fornicated ——
**Rector** — carnal lusts and appetites ——
**Isobel** — they — for — ni — cated ——
**Rector** — like brute beasts ——
**Isobel** — in the library ——
**Rector** — like brute beasts who have ——
**Isobel** — fornicated!
**Rector** Lady Isobel, please! This is a church!
**Cressida** (*whispering intensely*) Mrs Hodge ...
**Mrs Hodge** Oh, ma'am — she can speak! A miracle! It's a miracle!
**Cressida** Get her out!
**Isobel** (*pounding the arm of her wheelchair*) Damn you ... damn you ...
**Mrs Hodge** Now, now, your ladyship — that's quite enough of that.

*Mrs Hodge wheels Isobel up the aisle and out of the church*

**Isobel** (*as she goes*) Damn ... you .... damn you ...

*The Rector waits for silence*

**Rector** (*forcing a smile*) Like brute beasts — or rather not like brute beasts — beasts that have no — no understanding. But reverently. Discreetly. Advisedly. Soberly. And in the fear of God.

*Richard and Cressida kneel on the stools, facing each other*

Therefore if any man can shew any just cause why they should not be ——

*Emily enters at the rear of the auditorium. Her hair is now crudely chopped shoulder-length in the manner of a Renaissance prince, and she wears black, Hamlet-like garb*

**Emily** I am a man. I am such a man. (*She approaches down the aisle*) Is murder just cause? Is fornication? This man murdered my father. Poisoned him. Poisoned him in the garden of his own estate. A crime so foul it stinks to heaven. (*She stands on a lower step, directly addressing the congregation*) And on the day of the funeral, the very day of my father's funeral — he fornicated with my mother. (*She looks back to the Rector*) Is this just cause?
**Richard** It's not true ... it's not true ...

*Cressida closes her eyes, covers her ears and moans. Richard tries to hold her*

**Cressida** Can't you hear? Don't you hear it?
**Richard** Hear what? Cressida ...?

*Terrified, Cressida suddenly pushes Richard away. She recovers and moves to Emily*

**Cressida** Your hair. Your beautiful hair. What have you done? What kind of game is this?
**Emily** He murdered Father!
**Cressida** No. No.
**Emily** Why won't you believe me?
**Cressida** (*holding Emily*) Richard's good and kind. Richard wouldn't hurt a fly.
**Emily** (*struggling*) Let me go! Let me go!
**Cressida** Darling, this is a church, this is God's house. How can I protect you, how can I protect you if you won't even ——
**Emily** Let me go!

*Emily bites Cressida's hand, pulls free and bolts up the aisle and out of the church*

**Cressida** Emily! Emily ...
**Richard** (*approaching, touching her*) Cressida ...

*Richard leads Cressida back to the altar where they kneel as before. But the Rector hesitates*

Get on with it; what's wrong with you, man? The girl's demented! Any damn fool can see that! Now get on with it! I said — get on with it!
**Rector** (*deciding to continue*) Richard Edward Harker: wilt thou have this woman to thy wedded wife?

Act II                                                                                              49

*There is the sound of distant thunder*

> Wilt thou love her, comfort her, honour and keep her, in sickness and in health, and forsaking all other keep thee only unto her, as long as ye both shall live?
> **Richard** I will.

*The sound of the thunder draws closer*

**Rector** Cressida Elizabeth Arlington: wilt thou have this man to thy wedded husband? Wilt thou obey him, serve him, love him, honour him, keep him in sickness and in health, forsaking all other, so long as ye both shall live?

*Cressida reaches for Richard's face, explores it. Richard gently takes her trembling hand and kisses it*

**Cressida** (*smiling*) I will. Yes, I will. Of course I will.
**Rector** I now pronounce you Man and Wife.

*Richard and Cressida stand and kiss*

> In the Name of the Father, and of the Son, and the Holy Ghost. Amen.

*There is a crash of thunder*

*Dr Shawcross, Aubrey, Dorothy, Mabel, the Rector, Cressida and Richard exit*

*Black-out*

*The sound of the cold wind rises and the golden cross glows in the dark*

*Beneath, a shaft of silver light illuminates Emily, her head lowered in prayer, kneeling in the manner of a medieval knight*

**Emily** They won't listen. They still won't listen. His spell charms them all. But he was frightened. Oh yes, he was frightened. No more the villain smiles, no more the serpent thrives. Yet he lives. He still lives. And now — now they are wed. Wed. Father's funeral, mother's wedding. Rather I met him in Heaven than face this day. My hair. My beautiful hair. Joan of Arc — Joan of Arc cut her hair. A saint. A saint, pure and perfect. They burned her. Pure and perfect, they still burned her. She heard God's voice ... O, Lord, save me! She heard your voice. Sweet Lord, she heard your voice. She heard your voice and they burned her.

**Voice** Revenge. Revenge thy father.
**Emily** Honour thy father, Revenge thy father.
**Voice** Honour thy father, Revenge thy father.
**Emily** Our Father, which art in Heaven, Hallowed be thy Name, Thy Kingdom come, Thy will be done. Thy will be done. (*She stands and stares at the cross*) Give me Thy strength, make me Thy instrument, and I will fight this evil, eye for eye, life for life. From this time forth my thoughts be bloody, or be nothing worth.

*She runs off*

*Black-out*

*The sound of the wind fades*

*The sound of a grandfather clock solemnly slices the silence. As it whirrs and chimes the hour, the Lights slowly rise on Richard, Cressida and Mrs Hodge, standing formally in line waiting to welcome the wedding guests. Mrs Hodge holds a silver tray of shivering sherry glasses. There is a pause*

*Richard checks his pocket-watch. There is another pause*

**Cressida** Richard ...
**Richard** Five minutes.
**Cressida** They're not coming.
**Richard** Five more minutes.
**Cressida** No-one's coming.
**Richard** We're married. Nothing else matters.
**Cressida** Half the village think you killed him. Doesn't that matter?
**Richard** They need evidence. The word of a lunatic is not evidence.
**Cressida** Please don't say that.
**Richard** It's the truth. You have to face it.
**Cressida** You don't understand. She invents things. She's never had a friend so she ——
**Richard** "... a crime so foul it stinks to Heaven?"
**Cressida** What?
**Richard** *Hamlet*. It's *Hamlet*.
**Mrs Hodge** That's right, sir: William Shakespeare. She loves that book, she does.
**Cressida** Richard, I don't feel well. I really don't think I can ——
**Richard** But don't you see? You're the Queen and I'm the wicked Uncle.
**Cressida** I'm sorry?
**Richard** I murder her father and I marry her mother.
**Mrs Hodge** (*crossing herself*) God forgive you, sir.

## Act II

**Richard** No, no, Mrs Hodge, what I meant was ——
**Mrs Hodge** He was a difficult man, sir, I know that. No-one knows that more than ... but murder ...
**Richard** Mrs Hodge ——

*Three thuds of a heavy door knocker are heard*

Mrs Hodge, I did not murder Lord Arlington!
**Mrs Hodge** Whatever you say, sir.
**Richard** Mrs Hodge, will you please understand ——
**Cressida** Richard ... I don't feel at all well. I really don't think I can ——

*Mabel and Dorothy enter. Mabel grips Richard's hand, eyes bright with excitement*

**Mabel** My dear boy — we're so sorry.
**Dorothy** So sorry.
**Mabel** Isn't it awful?
**Dorothy** Awful.
**Mabel** You must be feeling dreadful, absolutely dreadful.
**Dorothy** Dreadful.
**Mabel** And you, Cressida. You of course have our deepest sympathy.
**Dorothy** Oh yes, our deepest ——
**Cressida** Thank you.

*Dorothy bravely kisses Richard*

**Mabel** We don't think you're a murderer. Not for a moment. Do we, Dorothy?
**Dorothy** No, no ... not for a, not for a ...

*They back off and help themselves to sherry*

**Mabel** We think the dreadful child should be horse-whipped.
**Dorothy** Yes, horse-whipped. And so does Uncle George.
**Mabel** As if things weren't bad enough.
**Dorothy** And now they're so much worse.
**Cressida** Perhaps you'd like to go on through?
**Mabel** Yes, of course, my dear. Now, now — chin up. Amor winkie omnia, as we say. It's Latin, don't you know. Come along, Dorothy ...

*They exit*

(*Off*) Ah, Aubrey — there you are! Isn't it dreadful? Perfectly awful. We were just saying how dreadful it all is.

*There is a pause*

**Richard**  It fits. It all fits. There's even a ghost.
**Cressida**  Ghost?
**Richard**  That's why she cut her hair. That's why she was wearing that ridiculous costume. Hamlet! She thinks she's Hamlet!
**Cressida**  I — I don't believe I've read *Hamlet*.
**Richard**  You haven't read *Hamlet*? But darling, you must. I mean, it's not only perhaps the greatest ——
**Cressida**  How does it end?
**Richard**  Hm?
**Cressida**  End. How does it end?
**Richard**  Oh ... Well, after a long time thinking about it, Hamlet finally decides to ...

*Pause*

**Cressida**  To what?
**Richard**  To — to take revenge, and ——
**Cressida**  Take revenge and what?
**Richard**  Well, everyone — almost everyone dies.
**Cressida**  But that's terrible.
**Richard**  It is a tragedy.
**Cressida**  How? How do they die?
**Richard**  Poison.
**Cressida**  Poison?
**Richard**  At least that's how ... but surely, surely you don't, you don't think ——?

*There is a sudden penetrating scream from the dining-room. Mrs Hodge almost drops her tray. Cressida and Richard exchange looks of abject horror*

**Cressida**  The sherry! Richard, the sherry!

*Another scream*

**Richard**  Oh my God ...

*Dorothy rushes on, a hand covering her quivering mouth*

The sherry. Did you drink the sherry?

Act II                                                                 53

**Cressida**  Dorothy — did you drink the sherry?
**Dorothy**  A penis!
**Richard**  A what?
**Cressida**  What did she say?

*Mabel rushes on, similarly distressed*

**Mabel**  The groom! The groom is a pig with a penis!
**Richard**  I beg your pardon!
**Dorothy**  A huge penis!
**Cressida**  Mabel, will you please ——
**Mabel**  A penis, Cressida! As bold as you like!
**Dorothy**  A pig with a penis!
**Cressida**  Of course he has a penis, all men have a penis, but that's hardly reason to insult him! There's no shame in a man having ——
**Mabel**  No, no — the table! On top of the cake!
**Cressida**  Richard, is it me, or are the frustrated old prunes completely ——?
**Mabel**  Frustrated old prunes!
**Dorothy**  The cake, Cressida! It was on top of the cake!
**Cressida**  What was?
**Dorothy**  This! (*She produces a model pig, dancing on its hind legs, displaying a preposterous phallus*) This sacrilege!
**Mabel**  Pagan sacrilege!

*Cressida laughs, almost hysterical*

  Are you determined to make a mockery of marriage!
**Cressida**  Oh, look! Look, Richard ——
**Mabel**  It's disgusting!
**Dorothy**  Obscene!
**Cressida**  Look what she's done!
**Mabel**  It could be the Devil himself!
**Richard**  Thank God! Thank God! (*He kisses the pig*) Hallelujah!
**Dorothy**  Oh!
**Richard**  Praise the Lord!
**Mabel**  What!
**Richard**  No, no, I mean — I mean we don't mean ——
**Cressida**  It's Emily — she plays games, it's just one of her ——
**Richard**  You see, we thought — we thought you'd both been poisoned.
**Mabel**  Poisoned?
**Dorothy**  Poisoned!
**Richard**  I know it sounds funny, but when we heard ——
**Mabel**  You find the prospect amusing?
**Richard**  No, no, of course not, it's just that ——

**Mabel** The man's a maniac!
**Richard** No, no, you don't understand.
**Mabel** We must leave this place at once! Dorothy — back to Bridlington!
**Dorothy** Bridlington!
**Richard** No, no, wait, wait! Ladies, please! (*He touches Dorothy*)

*Dorothy screams*

>   Will you calm down! Will you please calm down. Will you both, please ——!

*Mabel attacks Richard*

*Aubrey enters from downstage and observes the struggle*

**Mabel** Unhand her, you fiend! You — you breeder of swine!
**Richard** Stupid old trout, I'm only trying to ——
**Mabel** How dare you! (*She slaps his cheek*)
**Dorothy** Yes, how dare you! (*She slaps his other cheek*)
**Mabel** We always knew you lacked quality, Mr Harker. But we never imagined you were in league with the Devil!
**Richard** Well if I am — I can't wait to see you both in hell!

*Mabel and Dorothy squeal and exit*

*Richard stands dazed. Cressida has almost exhausted her sanity*

**Cressida** Will you please excuse me?
**Richard** Cressida ...?
**Cressida** I'm fine. Don't worry. I'm perfectly fine.

*She slowly exits upstage*

*Richard watches her go, helpless*

**Aubrey** Can I have a word, old man?

*A bell rings, off, continuing under the following*

**Richard** What's that?
**Mrs Hodge** Lady Isobel, sir. Shall I go and —— ?
**Richard** Yes. Yes, of course.
**Mrs Hodge** (*heading for the exit*) Drop more brandy, that'll shut her up.

*She exits*

Act II                                                                                                  55

**Aubrey** Richard?
**Richard** Hm? Oh. I'm sorry, Aubrey. It'll have to wait. (*He turns away and begins to climb the steps*)
**Aubrey** It is rather important.
**Richard** Yes, I'm sure. I'm sure it is. But so is Cressida ...

*The Lights slowly fade to Black-out*

*Aubrey exits*

*The bell stops ringing*

*The Lights rise on Cressida, sitting on the edge of the raised platform, holding a pillow*

**Cressida** Pig ... hypocritical, sanctimonious fat old pig, haven't you tortured me enough? There's nothing you can do worse than before. Nothing. Filthy, dirty ... you know I hate you, you know I hate you and you still, you still ... I am not evil! I'm not, I'm not! Don't care, I don't care — if you're in Heaven, I'd sooner be in Hell. No ... no ... no such place, no such place. Strong.

*Richard approaches*

Must be strong, I must be —— (*She looks up and sees Richard. She puts the pillow to one side*) I want to be on my own. I need to be on my own.
**Richard** Why here? Why Toby's room?
**Cressida** I want him to go away. I was telling him to go away.
**Richard** Telling who? Cressida ...?
**Cressida** I should never have married you.
**Richard** Darling, you're overwrought and you need to rest. Come on, let me take you to your room ——
**Cressida** I've told you. I have to stay.
**Richard** (*sighing and sitting*) We can't afford to act as if we're guilty.
**Cressida** We are guilty.
**Richard** What are we going to do about Emily?
**Cressida** Have they found her?
**Richard** Not yet. But when they do, don't you think she'd be better somewhere — somewhere more secure, more safe?
**Cressida** Oh, no ...
**Richard** We have no choice.
**Cressida** Don't you think I feel wretched enough?
**Richard** And what about Isobel? You do realize she must have seen us?

**Cressida** Don't be stupid.
**Richard** The library, in the library, that's what she said.
**Cressida** If she'd seen us in the library, I think she'd have mentioned it at the time.
**Richard** How else could she know?
**Cressida** Toby. Toby told her.
**Richard** Toby?
**Cressida** He's here. He's still here.
**Richard** Cressida ...
**Cressida** This is his punishment. He's using Emily to destroy us.
**Richard** You mean he's risen from the grave and he's now twisting the mind of his own daughter just to make our lives a little more miserable? Is that it? Well, at least it's in character ...
**Cressida** Oh yes, it's in character.
**Richard** The only thing that's destroying us is your guilt. All those years of fire and damnation — haven't you had enough?
**Cressida** Don't you remember? That night we played bridge. His ghost. Emily saw his ghost.
**Richard** It was a dream; you said so yourself!
**Cressida** In the garden, when you kissed me in the garden, I saw him too.
**Richard** You saw him? You mean he was actually — what? Standing there watching us?
**Cressida** He's still here. Sometimes — sometimes I even ——
**Richard** Is he here now? Well? Is he? Hallo! Is there anybody there?
**Cressida** Stop it!
**Richard** Let's call his bluff, shall we? Toby Arlington — calling Lord Arlington. Can you hear me?
**Cressida** Don't. Please don't.
**Richard** Come out, come out, wherever you are! Come on, you pompous, self-righteous bigot — show yourself. There. You see? Nothing. Nothing but dust and gloom. Ah! But wait!
**Cressida** Richard ...
**Richard** Something wicked this way comes. Do I hear the rattle of chains?

*Pause*

**Cressida** It's not like that.
**Richard** No, it's damn well not. Which is why we need to be rather more down-to-earth. Emily has to be certified. Yes, Cressida. And soon. The more we delay, the more plausible she'll seem. Even Aubrey's suspicious.
**Cressida** Aubrey's a friend.
**Richard** He's also a retired police inspector.
**Cressida** No, no, he'd never ——

Act II                                                              57

**Richard**  Wouldn't he? I don't share your confidence.
**Cressida**  I love you both. How can you ask me to choose?
**Richard**  Her mad tongue could send me to the gallows. Send us both. Now will you please ——

*Mrs Hodge rushes in, distraught*

**Mrs Hodge**  Sir ... sir ...
**Richard**  Yes, Mrs Hodge?
**Mrs Hodge**  Sir, something strange, something really strange ——
**Cressida**  What is it?
**Mrs Hodge**  Lady Isobel, ma'am. I've had to send for the doctor.
**Richard**  Now what?
**Mrs Hodge**  I think she's dying, sir.
**Richard**  Wonderful!
**Cressida**  Richard!
**Richard**  I was trying to be ironic. No, I wasn't.
**Mrs Hodge**  But, sir. It's not her, sir.
**Richard**  What's not her?
**Cressida**  For heaven's sake, woman — what's happened?
**Mrs Hodge**  I only wish I knew, ma'am. When I got to her room, she was, well ... all agitated. I tried my best to calm her, but she'd have none of it. You've never seen the like, she just kept pointing ——
**Cressida**  Pointing?
**Richard**  Pointing at what?
**Mrs Hodge**  A chair, sir. Only it was as if — as if she was seeing something.
**Richard**  Of course she was seeing something, she was seeing the damn chair!
**Cressida**  Richard, please.
**Mrs Hodge**  It was like there was someone sitting there.
**Richard**  Sitting in the empty chair?
**Mrs Hodge**  That's right, sir.
**Richard**  Someone invisible?
**Mrs Hodge**  Well they'd have to be, sir, wouldn't they? Otherwise I'd have seen them.
**Richard**  So tell me, Mrs Hodge, how exactly do you tell the difference between a chair which is empty and a chair which has someone invisible sitting in it?
**Mrs Hodge**  Well, sir. It's hard to put into words.
**Richard**  I can imagine. But perhaps you'd like to try?
**Mrs Hodge**  Well, sir — it's like a feeling.
**Richard**  Oh — a feeling?
**Cressida**  Did you see anything?

**Mrs Hodge**  No, ma'am.
**Richard**  There. She saw nothing. It was an empty chair and she saw nothing. Now will you both ——
**Mrs Hodge**  But I did hear something, sir.
**Richard**  Don't tell me — the rattle of chains?
**Mrs Hodge**  It was a rattle all right, sir. But not chains. It was what they call the death rattle. I've only heard it the once, when my father passed over, but once heard, you never forget. Oh, no. Breathing, it is. But not normal ... not normal breathing. It starts soft as a whisper but then it starts to strain and choke, half dead, half alive, as it struggles for each and every ——
**Richard**  Yes, thank you, Mrs Hodge.
**Mrs Hodge**  Well sir. That's what I heard, sir.
**Richard**  You heard Lady Isobel.
**Mrs Hodge**  Oh no, sir, it was like nothing you've ever ——
**Richard**  You heard Lady Isobel.
**Mrs Hodge**  If you say so, sir, only ...
**Richard**  Only what?
**Mrs Hodge**  Well, sir: it sounded like a man.
**Cressida**  Toby. It was Toby.
**Mrs Hodge**  Sorry, ma'am?
**Richard**  That'll be all.
**Mrs Hodge**  You mean his lordship ——?
**Richard**  Mrs Hodge, that will be all.
**Mrs Hodge**  As you wish, sir. Oh, sir: Mr Aubrey's still waiting.
**Richard**  I'll be down in a minute.
**Mrs Hodge**  Very good, sir.

*She leaves*

*There is a pause*

**Cressida**  Now do you believe me?
**Richard**  She heard Isobel.
**Cressida**  No she didn't. And you know it.

*There is a pause. Richard chuckles*

I fail to see what you can possibly find amusing ——
**Richard**  I'm sorry. Just a thought, a silly ——
**Cressida**  What?
**Richard**  Nothing.
**Cressida**  Tell me ...
**Richard**  (*adopting a Shakespearian attitude*) Toby. Or not Toby. That is the question.

# Act II

**Cressida** Is that meant to be funny?
**Richard** I thought a little levity might ——
**Cressida** Levity? You insensitive ——
**Richard** Cressida — the dead are dead and the dead stay dead!

*Cressida hands Richard the key and storms towards the exit during the following*

**Cressida** Fool! Bloody fool! Here! Lock the door! Lock the door and keep it locked!

*She storms off*

*Richard stands a moment, his eyes searching the gloom*

*Mrs Hodge enters, startling Richard*

**Mrs Hodge** I do beg your pardon, sir. Only her ladyship insists this room's kept locked. Are you all right, sir?
**Richard** (*handing her the key*) It's been a difficult day.

*He leaves. Mrs Hodge looks round a moment, then hurries off*

*Black-out*

*The Lights rise on Aubrey, pacing impatiently. He pauses by a window (This is imaginary)*

*Richard enters*

**Richard** Sorry to keep you.

*Mrs Hodge enters carrying a tray with a bottle of whisky and a couple of glasses*

As I'm sure you can imagine, Cressida's rather upset.
**Aubrey** Indeed I can.
**Richard** (*to Mrs Hodge*) Just leave it, would you?

*Mrs Hodge puts the tray on the raised platform and leaves*

Will you join me?
**Aubrey** No, thank you.

**Richard** Oh. Not like you. (*He pours a stiff Scotch*) Still no sign of Emily. Where will she go?

**Aubrey** The woods. She usually hides in the woods.

**Richard** I didn't realize she was so — so ill. What a day, eh? God, I hate this place. It's like living in a morgue. Or an asylum. Cheers. What's wrong, old chum? Lost for words?

**Aubrey** It is rather delicate.

**Richard** What is?

**Aubrey** Emily has made certain allegations.

**Richard** Allegations? That sounds rather formal.

**Aubrey** Were you and Cressida having an affair?

**Richard** I hardly think it any of your business.

**Aubrey** Richard, I've always considered you a friend ——

**Richard** And I you, Aubrey. But tell me — are you now speaking as a friend? Or as the Great Detective?

**Aubrey** Both.

**Richard** I see.

**Aubrey** Well?

**Richard** This is outrageous! How can you even ... Cressida is the most virtuous of women! It pains me you even ask.

**Aubrey** And so the day — the day of the funeral — that wasn't true?

**Richard** I'll humour your questions, but I'm damned if I'll be insulted. Nor will I have Cressida's reputation ——

**Aubrey** Was it true?

**Richard** Aubrey, the girl's deranged, demented, insane. Has it not occurred to you why she was wearing that ridiculous costume? Well?

**Aubrey** You mean Hamlet?

**Richard** Yes, I mean Hamlet. Don't you see? What with her grief, and her fevered imagination ... well, she's lost her mind, all sense of reality ——

**Aubrey** Is it likely she could invent such a thing?

**Richard** Fantasy! Sexual fantasy! It's her age. I thought you understood something of psychology?

**Aubrey** She's always been a child of fantasy, but something like this ... something must have triggered it. Something quite shocking. What I believe Freud would call a trauma.

**Richard** Yes ... possibly. Quite likely, in fact. But since we'll never know, I'm sure you'll agree, what's important now is we find her the very best available treatment. Now if you don't mind, Aubrey ... it's getting rather late and I have had a somewhat taxing ——

**Aubrey** I was thinking how distressed she was that day.

**Richard** What day?

**Aubrey** The day of her father's funeral. Don't you remember? That outburst ...

Act II                                                    61

**Richard**  Of course I remember.
**Aubrey**  So do I. Quite vividly, in fact. Cressida went off to look for her. And so, I recall, did you ...?
**Richard**  And so did several others ...
**Aubrey**  I went upstairs to her room. Where did you go?
**Richard**  The garden. I searched the garden.
**Aubrey**  Did you see Cressida?
**Richard**  How could I? She was searching the house. As you well know.
**Aubrey**  And you didn't have occasion to go into the library?
**Richard**  No, I did not.
**Aubrey**  You're absolutely certain?
**Richard**  Of course I'm certain.
**Aubrey**  You give me your word?
**Richard**  Don't be absurd! How many more times ——?
**Aubrey**  Do you give me your word?
**Richard**  Yes, my word, you have my word!

*There is a pause*

**Aubrey**  I saw you, Richard. I saw you go into the library with my own eyes. Naturally, I didn't think anything of it. Until today.

*There is a pause*

**Richard**  All right ... all right, it's true, but ——
**Aubrey**  Is it any wonder she despises you? Have you no sense of shame whatsoever?
**Richard**  (*pouring himself another Scotch*) We were in love, it's what people do when ——
**Aubrey**  For heaven's sake, man — we'd only just buried him!
**Richard**  Cressida said it was the happiest day of her life.
**Aubrey**  Oh, I see — all her doing, was it?
**Richard**  However regrettable, however reprehensible, it was not a crime.
**Aubrey**  That's sure to win the hearts and minds of a jury.
**Richard**  Jury? What do you mean — jury?
**Aubrey**  Means. Opportunity. And now motive. It doesn't look good, does it?

*There is a pause*

**Richard**  No. No, it doesn't. Yes, you're right. Looked at from the outside — if it ... if it ever came to court, well, anything, anything could happen. And as for Cressida ...
**Aubrey**  Quite.

**Richard** It would destroy her. She'd be ruined. And all because of me. The things we do, eh? Listen, Aubrey ... I'm not trying to excuse myself, but you're a man of experience. Have you never loved a woman so much you'd risk anything to have her? When I first met Cressida I felt as if I'd fallen off the edge of the world. It was wrong, I know it was wrong even to hope ——
**Aubrey** Adultery, deception, betrayal.
**Richard** Yes, yes all that, I confess to all that. But once I'd learned the truth of her miserable marriage, I simply couldn't help myself. Denying love is surely an even greater wrong? Try and understand, she captivated my every second thought. My love for her meant more to me than life itself.
**Aubrey** And what of Toby? What of his life?
**Richard** Are you accusing me?
**Aubrey** Did you kill him, Richard? Did you kill Toby?
**Richard** I was his friend, damn it!
**Aubrey** And so you made love with his wife?
**Richard** I am not a murderer! It's *Hamlet*! Why won't you understand? The girl's deranged, deluded ——
**Aubrey** Blaming her won't save your skin either. Mrs Hodge said you confessed.
**Richard** I did no such thing! Aubrey, please ——
**Aubrey** How could I have been such a fool? You've betrayed me.
**Richard** Aubrey ...
**Aubrey** I trusted you with everything I hold dear and you betrayed me.
**Richard** This is madness.
**Aubrey** Good-night. (*He makes as if to leave*)
**Richard** (*restraining Aubrey*) At least think of Cressida ...
**Aubrey** You think of Cressida. If you really care, you could spare her by pleading guilty.
**Richard** But I'm not. Aubrey, I'm not.
**Aubrey** Will you get out of my way!

*Richard stands aside and Aubrey leaves*

*Richard stares into his drink*

*Mrs Hodge enters*

**Mrs Hodge** Begging your pardon, sir: Cook wants to know what to do with all the food?
**Richard** Not now.
**Mrs Hodge** As you wish, sir. Only it seems a sin to waste so much ——
**Richard** Get out! Just get out!

Act II                                                                                      63

**Mrs Hodge** Very good, sir.

*She leaves*

*Richard broods a little longer and pours another drink*

*Dr Shawcross enters, unnoticed. He coughs*

**Doctor** I've, er ... I've given her a sedative.
**Richard** How is she?
**Doctor** Dying. Thank God.
**Richard** Whisky?
**Doctor** Not for me. Tell you the truth, my concern is more for Cressida. I hoped I might have a wee word?
**Richard** She's asleep.
**Doctor** I see. Well, if you're sure ...
**Richard** I'm sure.
**Doctor** Right then — I shall be on my way.
**Richard** But I do want you to certify Emily.
**Doctor** Is that what Cressida wants?
**Richard** It's what we both want. It wasn't an easy decision, but ... well, there it is. Emily needs to be certified. Certified and committed. A few months hopefully, just until ... until she gets better.
**Doctor** I shall have to think about that.
**Richard** Are you suggesting she's sane?
**Doctor** I'm far from certain she's mad.
**Richard** Meaning what precisely?
**Doctor** Meaning we'll talk about it tomorrow.
**Richard** You as well, eh?
**Doctor** Richard, I'm a doctor, not a ——
**Richard** Yes, you're a doctor — you performed the autopsy. Food poisoning, that's what you said.
**Doctor** So it appeared at the time.
**Richard** So it appeared at the time. I nearly died, damn it! Do you think I'd deliberately poison myself?
**Doctor** If you were clever and desperate enough ——
**Richard** Oh, thank you. Thank you very much. If you say that in court, I'm as good as dead.
**Doctor** Which is why I need to think. We'll talk tomorrow.
**Richard** Do you believe in ghosts?
**Doctor** Why? Have you seen one?
**Richard** Cressida thinks Emily's possessed. By her father's spirit. That all this ... all this is Toby's revenge. Isn't that ridiculous?

**Doctor** Should you not be talking to the rector?
**Richard** Good God, no; he'd probably believe her. Like you, Doctor, I believe we create our own gods and demons. Trouble is, I'm beginning to wonder if I might be wrong. It seems like all the Arlington ghosts have been resurrected in the mind of that poor sick girl, haunting her with all their hate and superstition. And now all that hate is being turned against me. No matter what I do or what I say, no-one believes me and everything conspires against me. But I am innocent, I swear to God I'm innocent. I broke the rules, I broke all the rules. But I did not kill him.
**Doctor** Ay well, that'll be for the court to decide.
**Richard** Is that all you have to say?
**Doctor** I could say how much you disgust me for taking advantage of a poor widow woman at the time of her greatest grief, but since it wouldn't do a ha'p'orth of good, I shan't waste my breath.
**Richard** She hated him.
**Doctor** They were married. They were married, and there's an end of it. I'll find my own way out.

*Dr Shawcross leaves*

*Richard pours another drink and swigs*

**Richard** (*muttering*) What to do, what to do?

*The Lights snap out*

*Richard exits*

*The Lights rise on Cressida, now wearing a nightdress, brushing her hair as she sits on a stool in front of an imaginary dressing-table, humming softly to herself*

*Richard enters, jacketless, unbuttoning his shirt*

I think we should take a holiday.
**Cressida** Oh yes, I'd love a proper honeymoon.
**Richard** Tomorrow. First thing.
**Cressida** Tomorrow?
**Richard** With or without Emily.
**Cressida** Darling, I've told you: once we've found a suitable school ——
**Richard** We'll make sure she's well taken care of ...
**Cressida** We can't just leave her. Not when she's — when she's — besides, whatever will people think?
**Richard** No worse than they're thinking already.

Act II 65

**Cressida** Oh, it'll pass ... a few weeks, you'll see.
**Richard** No, it won't. I think Aubrey plans to consult some of his former colleagues.

*There is a pause*

**Cressida** Very well. Tomorrow. We'll leave tomorrow.
**Richard** Thank you. (*He kisses Cressida's neck*) Let's go to bed ...

*The sound of the laboured breathing of a dying man comes up slowly*

*Cressida stares at the mirror, recoils*

**Richard** What's wrong?
**Cressida** The mirror ... look in the mirror ...
**Richard** There's nothing. There's only you and ——

*Cressida pulls away, moves downstage, hands covering her head*

**Cressida** He's here ... he's here ...
**Richard** Watching us? In the mirror — was he watching us? (*He holds Cressida*) Cressida, tell me ...
**Cressida** Can't ... I can't ... it's beyond all reason.
**Richard** (*forcing her to face him*) Now listen. We have enough problems without ——
**Cressida** (*attacking him, lashing viciously with the hairbrush*) Go away ... go away ... go away ... (*She hits him in the face with the brush*)
**Richard** (*moaning, turning his back, holding his injured face*) For God's sake!

*Cressida regains control; the sound of the breathing fades to silence*

**Cressida** (*moving to Richard*) Darling, I'm sorry ... I'm sorry ...
**Richard** My eye ...
**Cressida** I'm so sorry ...
**Richard** You hit my eye ...
**Cressida** I thought, I thought ...
**Richard** What? Thought what?

*Pause*

**Cressida** I thought you were him. I thought you were Toby.

*Exasperated, Richard sighs and sits*

I'm not mad. I'm not. I know that's what you think, but I'm not. This is his punishment. Yes, Richard — the worst thing in the world.

**Richard** Cressida ...

**Cressida** When we make love, it's like — like a dance. But with him ... I used to think of you. Every time he used me, I'd fill my mind with you. But now ... now don't you see? God's turned it against me. This is his punishment.

**Richard** (*standing*) Stop it!

**Cressida** He won't let me love you, he won't: I can never love you.

**Richard** (*holding her and trying to force eye-contact*) Look at me. Look at me!

**Cressida** I killed him. Richard, I killed him.

*There is a pause*

**Richard** (*releasing Cressida*) You killed Toby?

**Cressida** He was dying. Day after day I watched him die. Each day I felt stronger, closer to freedom. But then — then he began to get better and I couldn't bear it. I couldn't. I just couldn't, I couldn't bear it. It was like a dream. I picked up the pillow — I picked up the pillow and I just watched myself do it. As if it were someone else. For you — I did it for you ...

**Richard** For me?

**Cressida** I love you, I love you.

*Richard turns away and sits, cradling his head*

**Richard** You had no right!

**Cressida** I had every right! He'd been killing me for years. Do you imagine I ever wanted to marry such a man? The moment I saw him, I loathed him. I was seventeen. Seventeen, Richard; scarcely more than a child. Mama locked me in my room until I consented: no food, no water, nothing. It was a good match, you see, a very good match and Mama was very determined. I lasted three days.

**Richard** That's monstrous — little better than slavery.

**Cressida** Not slavery. I wasn't his slave, I was his whore.

*There is a pause*

**Richard** It's still murder, Cressida.

**Cressida** How many times did you wish him dead? How many times did you dream of stealing his life, his home, his money, his bed? Well? Cat caught your tongue?

**Richard** What's happening to us ——

**Cressida** The sin is in the thought, not the deed.

# Act II

**Richard** That's not true.
**Cressida** Of course, it's true; it's in the Bible.
**Richard** That doesn't make it true. We all think terrible things, but if we acted on them ... America. We'll go to America. It's our only chance. First thing tomorrow, we'll ——

*Cressida breathes erratically, terrified. Richard goes to her*

    Cressida ...? Is he — is he here now?

*She nods, too frightened to look at him*

    Cressida ...
**Cressida** Don't ... please, don't ... keep away, please keep away ...

*The sound of the laboured breathing of a dying man slowly fades up*

    You hear it? You can hear it?

*The breathing rises in volume, filling the room*

**Richard** Cressida, look at me ...
**Cressida** No ...
**Richard** Whatever this thing is, you have to confront it.

*She turns to look at him and recoils in horror*

    If I can forgive you, I'm sure God can. Now look at me.
**Cressida** Can't ... I can't ...
**Richard** Trust me ... you have to trust me.

*She turns again to face him*

    It's me. It's only me. Good, that's good. Now hold me ... hold me ...

*She enters his embrace*

    Let it pass, let it pass ...

*The breathing stops*

    Gone?
**Cressida** Gone.

*There is a pause*

**Emily** (*singing; off*) Row, row, row the boat
                Gently down the stream
**Cressida** Emily ...
**Emily** (*off*)       Merrily, merrily, merrily, merrily
**Cressida** She's in the house.
**Emily** (*off*)       Life is but a dream.
**Richard** You check upstairs ...

*They exit*

*As they do so, the Lights fade to Black-out*

**Emily** (*off*)       Row, row, row the boat
                Gently down the stream

*We hear Richard and Cressida calling from different parts of the house*

**Cressida** (*off*) Emily!
**Richard** (*off*) Emily!
**Emily** (*off*)       Merrily, merrily, merrily, merrily
                Life is but a dream ...

*We hear the cold wind blowing; as it does, a shaft of silver moonlight slowly rises. The room is shadowy*

        (*Closer*) Row, row, row the boat
                Gently down the ... (*She stops*)
**Cressida** (*off; distant*) Emily ...
**Richard** (*off; much closer*) Emily ... ? Emily, please ...
**Emily** (*off*) ... merrily, merrily, merrily —— (*she stops abruptly*)

*Richard enters downstage*

**Richard** Emily? Emily, I know you're in here. Please, Emily — we have to talk ...

*There is a pause*

**Emily** (*off; upstage*) Merrily, merrily, merrily, merrily ...
**Richard** Emily ... (*His eyes search the room*) Emily ... all I want is for us to ——

## Act II

*Emily appears upstage, still in her Hamlet garb, holding a double-barrelled shotgun*

**Emily** Merrily, merrily, merrily, merrily ——

*Richard slowly turns to face his Nemesis*

— life is but a — dream.

*The sound of the cold wind dies away*

**Richard** For God's sake — what do you — what do you think you're ——?

*The bell rings incessantly. Emily raises her gun*

Emily ...

*She approaches*

(*Backing off*) Emily, these games really have to stop.
**Emily** It is the Day of Judgement.
**Richard** Emily, I am not a demon and I am not a devil. I'm an ordinary man, an ordinary, common man. Yes, I made love with your mother but I did not — I did not kill your father. Nor am I the King of Denmark. Now in the name of reason, will you please put down the gun.
**Emily** Vengeance is mine, saith the Lord.
**Richard** Thou shalt not kill!
**Emily** I am the Lord's annointed.
**Richard** Emily ...
**Emily** Die, demon ...

*She fires; a surreal, echoing acoustic*

*In slow-motion, Richard reels, twists and turns, before collapsing at the foot of the steps. (A strobe light could be effective here)*

**Emily** (*standing over Richard, rubbing her hurt shoulder*) No more the villain smiles.

*Cressida rushes on upstage. The bell stops ringing*

You're free. I've broken the spell.

*Cressida's eyes are drawn to her lover's lifeless body*

**Cressida** My God ... oh, my God ... what have you done? (*She cradles Richard*) My love ... my sweet love ...
**Emily** He killed father.
**Cressida** He was innocent!
**Emily** He was evil. God guided me, sent me signs ...
**Cressida** Stupid girl ... stupid, stupid ...
**Emily** Vengeance is mine, saith the Lord. I am his instrument.
**Richard** (*whispering*) The gun ... get the gun ...
**Cressida** Thank God ...
**Richard** Get the gun ...

*Emily points the shotgun at Richard and Cressida*

*Cressida looks up and sees Emily*

**Emily** He won't die. Why won't he die?
**Cressida** (*rising*) Emily ... it wasn't him.
**Emily** He's evil, a devil and a demon, that's why. Mother, why can't you ——?
**Cressida** Emily Arlington, you are my daughter and I love you very much. But if you don't stop this now, I shall have you certified and sent to the asylum. Yes, Emily — the asylum! Once there, you will be locked away for the rest of your life. Do you understand? The rest of your life. Now give me that gun.
**Emily** (*handing over the gun*) I still think he's a demon.
**Cressida** (*helping Richard to his feet*) Are you all right?
**Richard** I seem to be alive ...

*Mrs Hodge enters in her dressing-gown, carrying an oil-lamp*

**Mrs Hodge** What's happened ma'am? I heard an almighty — oh, my goodness ...
**Emily** I had to, Mrs Hodge. God told me.
**Mrs Hodge** God told you what, Miss Emily?
**Cressida** (*handing the gun to Mrs Hodge*) Never you mind. Will you please return this.

*There are three thuds from the door knocker*

*Richard looks knowingly at Cressida and dusts himself down*

**Richard** Now I wonder who that can be?
**Cressida** Oh, Richard ...

*Another three thuds*

Act II                                                                   71

**Richard** Aren't you going to answer it, Mrs Hodge?
**Mrs Hodge** This time of night, sir?
**Richard** Answer it.

*Mrs Hodge goes off*

**Cressida** Richard ...

*They embrace*

**Richard** Stay calm, keep calm.
**Cressida** Love you.
**Richard** And I love you.
**Cressida** Forever and ever?
**Richard** Forever and ever ...

*They kiss*

*Mrs Hodge returns with Aubrey, Inspector Eaton and a uniformed Police Officer. Mrs Hodge exits*

*Emily rushes to Aubrey*

*The lovers begin to sway to the rhythm of an imaginary waltz. Aubrey coughs pointedly, but they ignore him*

*The Lights change and music swells. Richard sweeps Cressida into "The Emperor Waltz". They dance the full circumference of the stage ending with the kiss as the Lights change back to their previous state. Richard finally breaks the embrace*

Come in, gentlemen. I've been expecting you.

*Inspector Eaton composes himself and steps forward*

**Eaton** I'm Chief Inspector Eaton — and this is Sergeant Charlton.
**Richard** I don't know what you've been told, Inspector, but I should like to ——
**Eaton** Are you Richard Edward Harker?
**Richard** I am.
**Eaton** Richard Edward Harker, I have a warrant for your arrest. You are not obliged to say anything ——
**Richard** This is ridiculous, quite absurd. Do you really imagine the confused ravings of a young girl will stand as evidence?

**Eaton**  That's for the court to decide, sir.
**Richard**  But it's all supposition, nothing but conjecture, how can you possibly ——?
**Eaton**  Anything you do say will be taken down and ——
**Cressida**  No! No! It wasn't him!
**Richard**  Cressida!
**Cressida**  It was me! I killed him ... I killed Toby.

*After a pause, Richard chuckles, clapping his hands; he circles and applauds Cressida*

**Richard**  Isn't she wonderful? Isn't she astonishing? (*He goes to Emily*)

*Emily huddles closer to Aubrey for protection*

> Now do you see how powerful I am? How I weave my tangled web? I fooled everyone, didn't I? Didn't I, Emily? Everyone except you ...

**Cressida**  (*approaching angrily*) No! No, Richard!
**Richard**  (*ignoring her*) You were right — there was something rotten in the state of Denmark. That's why I cast my spell — my most marvellous magic spell — and now ... now she'll do anything I want ... (*He rises and touches Cressida's face*) Anything at all. She'd even sacrifice her life. Wouldn't you?
**Cressida**  You have no right.
**Richard**  (*taking her hands*) Then forgive me. Forgive me as I forgive you. It's over. Accept it. Accept it and pay the price.
**Cressida**  (*understanding; kissing his hand*) Forever and ever?
**Richard**  Forever and ever ... (*He turns to Emily*) Look after your mother. She couldn't help what happened. (*He looks at Aubrey*) Well, Aubrey, old man, old chum ... what can I say? Another triumph for the Great Detective. And perhaps a final chapter? Hm?
**Aubrey**  May God forgive you.
**Richard**  You will take care of Cressida?
**Aubrey**  Of course.
**Richard**  Well then, gentlemen ... (*He turns to Inspector Eaton*) I think I'm ready.
**Eaton**  Take charge of the prisoner, Sergeant.
**Charlton**  Sir. (*He administers handcuffs*)
**Cressida**  (*making for Richard*) Richard ...
**Eaton**  (*restraining Cressida*) It's better you don't, ma'am. Take him away.
**Charlton**  Don't make it difficult, sir.
**Richard**  (*forcing a final smile*) Goodbye, my love.

*Eaton, Charlton and Richard leave. After a pause, Mrs Hodge rushes on and bobs*

Act II

**Mrs Hodge** Excuse me, ma'am.
**Aubrey** Not now, Mrs Hodge.
**Mrs Hodge** But, sir ——
**Aubrey** I said not now.

*Mrs Hodge waits, observing*

*Aubrey and Emily move downstage to comfort Cressida*

Cressida ... Can you ever forgive me?
**Emily** (*hugging Cressida*) Don't be sad. You mustn't be sad. You should rejoice. Mother, rejoice. God has saved you.

*The Lights slowly fade to black as the sound of the cold wind rises. For a moment, the golden cross floats in the dark, then fades back into nothingness*

*The sound of the cold wind slowly fades into the night* ——

— *and the rest is silence*

CURTAIN

# FURNITURE AND PROPERTY LIST

## ACT I

*On stage*:
    Chair
    Rocking chair
    Stool
    Other chairs
    Book for **Aubrey**

*Off stage*:
    Book of Common Prayer (**Rector**)
    Tray of glasses of sherry (**Mrs Hodge**)
    Rag doll (**Emily**)
    Hairbrush (**Cressida**)
    Oil lamp (**Mrs Hodge**)
    Bridge table. *On it*: score pads (**Mrs Hodge**)
    Cards (**Mrs Hodge**)
    Candle (**Emily**)
    Gladstone bag (**Dr Shawcross**)
    Candles (**All**)

*Personal*:
    **Isobel**: walking stick (used throughout Act I)

## ACT II

*On stage*:
    As Act I except book

*Off stage*:
    Book (**Emily**)
    Posy of wild flowers (**Cressida**)
    Tray of glasses of sherry (**Mrs Hodge**)
    Model pig with preposterous phallus (**Mabel**)
    Pillow (**Cressida**)
    Tray with bottle of whisky and glasses (**Mrs Hodge**)
    Hairbrush (**Cressida**)
    Double-barrelled shotgun (**Emily**)
    Oil lamp (**Mrs Hodge**)

*Personal*:
    **Richard**: pocket watch
    **Cressida**: key
    **Charlton**: handcuffs

Black Widow

*During black-out p.45*

*Set*:   Two small cushioned stools C
    Set of steps

*During black-out p.49*

*Strike*:   Cushioned stools
    Set of steps

# LIGHTING PLOT

ACT I

*To open*: Darkness

| | | |
|---|---|---|
| Cue 1 | Sounds of cold wind and bell<br>*Slowly bring up lights on cemetery area* | (Page 1) |
| Cue 2 | **Mabel**: "... Arlington virtues, are they not?"<br>*Dim lighting* | (Page 4) |
| Cue 3 | Sound of cold wind rises<br>*Fade to black-out* | (Page 5) |
| Cue 4 | Huge crash<br>*Shuddering white light on downstage chair* | (Page 5) |
| Cue 5 | **Dr Shawcross** laughs in the dark<br>*Bring up general lighting* | (Page 5) |
| Cue 6 | **Cressida**: "I'm ... I'm so sorry ..."<br>*Black-out* | (Page 10) |
| Cue 7 | Distant thunder<br>*Bring up pale pool of light on* **Emily** | (Page 10) |
| Cue 8 | **Cressida**: "Love you, love you, love you ..."<br>*Bring up light on higher level for* **Emily** | (Page 11) |
| Cue 9 | **Cressida**: "That's better ... much better ..."<br>*Bring up shuddering light on* **Emily** | (Page 12) |
| Cue 10 | When ready<br>*Black-out* | (Page 12) |
| Cue 11 | Storm fades to silence<br>*Bring up upstage lights on* **Cressida** *and* **Emily** | (Page 12) |
| Cue 12 | **Cressida**: "And I ... I shall pray for you."<br>*Fade lights to black* | (Page 13) |
| Cue 13 | **Mrs Hodge** enters with an oil lamp<br>*Bring up dim covering light (optional)* | (Page 13) |

| | | |
|---|---|---|
| Cue 14 | **Cressida** picks up the lamp and leads Isobel off<br>*Cut covering light; fade all lights to black-out* | (Page 15) |
| Cue 15 | **Aubrey**: " ... that I know ——"<br>*Bring up lighting on Aubrey and Emily* | (Page 15) |
| Cue 16 | **Emily** begins to read<br>*Lights change* | (Page 17) |
| Cue 17 | **Emily** returns to her book<br>*Lights slowly change again* | (Page 17) |
| Cue 18 | **Emily** and **Cressida**: " ... for I acknowledge my faults ... "<br>*Crossfade lights to downstage area with fireglow effect* | (Page 19) |
| Cue 19 | **Emily** enters carrying a candle<br>*Bring up dim covering light (optional)* | (Page 23) |
| Cue 20 | They take their places at the table<br>*Fade lights almost to black* | (Page 23) |
| Cue 21 | The sound of the wind rises<br>*Flicker light covering candle* | (Page 23) |
| Cue 22 | Laughter from downstage; the candle blows out<br>*Flicker light covering candle; snap off as candle is extinguished* | (Page 24) |
| Cue 23 | More laughter<br>*Slowly bring up lights on Bridge table* | (Page 24) |
| Cue 24 | **Cressida**: "Anyone care to join me?"<br>*Black-out; then bring up moonlight effect* | (Page 27) |
| Cue 25 | **Richard** and **Cressida** kiss<br>*Dim lights on Richard and Cressida so they are thrown into shadow* | (Page 28) |
| Cue 26 | **Richard**: "Cressida ... ?"<br>*Bring up moonlight on Richard and Cressida as before* | (Page 28) |
| Cue 27 | Startled, **Richard** looks round<br>*Black-out* | (Page 29) |
| Cue 28 | When ready<br>*Bring up light on Emily in rocking chair* | (Page 29) |

| | | |
|---|---|---|
| *Cue* 29 | **Dr Shawcross** leaves<br>*Fade lights on all but* **Emily** | (Page 31) |
| *Cue* 30 | **Emily** dances downstage<br>*Change lights for dance* | (Page 32) |
| *Cue* 31 | **Mrs Hodge**: " ... quite enough upset for one day."<br>*Fade lights, leaving* **Isobel** *silhouetted* | (Page 38) |
| *Cue* 32 | **Group** enters with candles<br>*Bring up covering light with individual spot*<br>    *on* **Emily** *(optional)* | (Page 38) |
| *Cue* 33 | **Emily** breathes out her candle<br>*Snap off spot on* **Emily** | (Page 39) |
| *Cue* 34 | **Cressida**: "Tonight? Why tonight?"<br>*Flicker light on candles; snap off as*<br>    *candles are extinguished* | (Page 40) |

ACT II

*To open*: Darkness

| | | |
|---|---|---|
| *Cue* 35 | Sound of cold wind blowing<br>*Bring up pool of light on* **Emily** | (Page 41) |
| *Cue* 36 | Sound of cold wind dies<br>*Bring up general lighting on stage* | (Page 41) |
| *Cue* 37 | **Aubrey** leads **Cressida** off<br>*Fade to black-out* | (Page 45) |
| *Cue* 38 | Church organ plays "Jesu, Joy of Man's Desiring"<br>*Bring up tight spot on golden cross and lights on*<br>    **Rector**, **Richard** *and* **Dr Shawcross** | (Page 45) |
| *Cue* 39 | All exit except Emily<br>*Black-out* | (Page 49) |
| *Cue* 40 | Sound of cold wind rises<br>*Bring up glow on golden cross and silver spot on* **Emily** | (Page 49) |
| *Cue* 41 | **Emily** runs off<br>*Black-out* | (Page 50) |

| | | |
|---|---|---|
| Cue 42 | Grandfather clock chimes the hour<br>*Lights slowly rise on* **Richard**, **Cressida** *and* **Mrs Hodge** | (Page 50) |
| Cue 43 | **Richard**: "But so is Cressida ... "<br>*Slowly fade to black-out* | (Page 55) |
| Cue 44 | Bell stops ringing<br>*Bring up light on* **Cressida** | (Page 55) |
| Cue 45 | **Mrs Hodge** hurries off<br>*Black-out; then bring up lights on* **Aubrey** | (Page 59) |
| Cue 46 | **Richard**: "What to do, what to do?"<br>*Snap to black-out; then bring up light on* **Cressida** | (Page 64) |
| Cue 47 | **Richard** and **Cressida** exit<br>*Fade to black-out* | (Page 68) |
| Cue 48 | Sound of wind blowing<br>*Bring up shaft of silver moonlight* | (Page 68) |
| Cue 49 | **Richard** reels, twists and turn, collapses<br>*Strobe (optional)* | (Page 69) |
| Cue 50 | **Mrs Hodge** enters carrying an oil lamp<br>*Bring up dim covering light (optional)* | (Page 70) |
| Cue 51 | **Aubrey** coughs<br>*Change lights to dance state* | (Page 71) |
| Cue 52 | Dance ends<br>*Revert lights to previous state* | (Page 71) |
| Cue 53 | **Emily**: "God has saved you."<br>*Slowly fade lights to black; bring up light on golden cross, then fade* | (Page 73) |

# EFFECTS PLOT

## ACT I

| | | |
|---|---|---|
| *Cue* 1 | As play opens<br>*Cold wind blowing; church bell tolling, fading<br>    as scene progresses* | (Page 1) |
| *Cue* 2 | **Mabel**: " ... Arlington virtues, are they not?"<br>*Distant thunder* | (Page 4) |
| *Cue* 3 | **Cressida** stands staring into the grave<br>*Increase volume of wind sound* | (Page 5) |
| *Cue* 4 | Lights slowly fade to black-out<br>*Thunder rumbles closer; then huge crash.<br>    Fade wind sound* | (Page 5) |
| *Cue* 5 | Black-out<br>*Distant thunder; storm sounds continue under scene* | (Page 10) |
| *Cue* 6 | **Cressida**: "That's better ... much better ... "<br>*More thunder* | (Page 12) |
| *Cue* 7 | Black-out<br>*Fade storm to silence* | (Page 12) |
| *Cue* 8 | **Emily** rocks the chair<br>*Bring up sound of cold wind* | (Page 17) |
| *Cue* 9 | **Cressida**: "Whatever do you mean, dead?"<br>*Fade sound of cold wind* | (Page 18) |
| *Cue* 10 | The Lights fade<br>*Slowly bring up the sound of the cold wind* | (Page 23) |
| *Cue* 11 | **Emily**: " ... waiting for the worms."<br>*Cold wind sound rises* | (Page 23) |
| *Cue* 12 | **Emily**: "Ay, old mole ... canst thou hear me?"<br>*Fade wind sound, then bring up electronically<br>    amplified man's sobbing (see p. 23)* | (Page 23) |

| | | |
|---|---|---|
| *Cue* 13 | **Emily**: "Papa? Papa ... ?"<br>*Sobbing stops* | (Page 23) |
| *Cue* 14 | **Emily** slowly nods<br>*Cold wind returns, rising and swelling* | (Page 24) |
| *Cue* 15 | The invisible force releases **Emily**'s hand<br>*Voice-over: dialogue as p. 24* | (Page 24) |
| *Cue* 16 | Candle flickers and blows out<br>*Fade cold wind sound* | (Page 24) |
| *Cue* 17 | Moonlight comes up<br>*A peacock screams* | (Page 27) |
| *Cue* 18 | A giant shadow smothers the lovers<br>*Bring up deep and laboured breathing of a dying man, becoming progressively more erratic* | (Page 28) |
| *Cue* 19 | **Richard**: "What's wrong? Cressida ... ?"<br>*Fade breathing sounds* | (Page 28) |
| *Cue* 20 | **Cressida** exits<br>*A peacock screams* | (Page 29) |
| *Cue* 21 | Lights fade<br>*Bring up sound of cold wind* | (Page 32) |
| *Cue* 22 | **Emily**: " ... go away ... "<br>*Fade sound of cold wind; bring up<br>  "The Emperor Waltz" faintly* | (Page 32) |
| *Cue* 23 | Lights change<br>*Increase volume of "The Emperor Waltz"* | (Page 32) |
| *Cue* 24 | **Isobel**: "And as for you ... as for you ... "<br>*Bring up sound of cold wind* | (Page 39) |
| *Cue* 25 | **Emily**: " ... and send them to Hell."<br>*Voice-over: dialogue as p. 39-40* | (Page 39) |
| *Cue* 26 | **Cressida**: "Tonight? Why tonight?"<br>*Increase volume of cold wind sound* | (Page 40) |

## ACT II

| | | |
|---|---|---|
| *Cue* 27 | As ACT II begins<br>*Sound of cold wind* | (Page 41) |

| | | |
|---|---|---|
| Cue 28 | **Emily**: "The readiness is all."<br>*Fade sound of cold wind* | (Page 41) |
| Cue 29 | **Aubrey** leads **Cressida** off; the lights fade<br>*"Jesu, Joy of Man's Desiring" on a church organ;*<br>*continue to cue from* **Rector** *p.46* | (Page 45) |
| Cue 30 | **Rector**: "Will you all please stand ..."<br>*Organ wheezes and plays "The Wedding March"* | (Page 46) |
| Cue 31 | **Mrs Hodge** crosses herself<br>*Music dies ignominiously* | (Page 46) |
| Cue 32 | **Mrs Hodge** escapes to the nearest seat<br>*"The Wedding March" plays again* | (Page 46) |
| Cue 33 | **Rector**: " ... thou have this woman to thy wedded wife?"<br>*Distant thunder* | (Page 48) |
| Cue 34 | **Richard**: "I will."<br>*Thunder draws closer* | (Page 49) |
| Cue 34 | **Rector**: " ... and the Holy Ghost. Amen."<br>*Crash of thunder* | (Page 49) |
| Cue 35 | Black-out<br>*Bring up sound of cold wind* | (Page 49) |
| Cue 36 | **Emily**: "She heard your voice and they burned her."<br>*Voice over: dialogue as p. 50* | (Page 50) |
| Cue 37 | Black-out<br>*Fade cold wind sound; bring up sound of grandfather*<br>*clock chiming the hour* | (Page 50) |
| Cue 38 | **Richard**: "Mrs Hodge ——"<br>*Three thuds of a heavy door knocker* | (Page 51) |
| Cue 39 | **Aubrey**: "Can I have a word, old man?"<br>*Bell rings and continues* | (Page 54) |
| Cue 40 | Black-out<br>*Cut bell sound* | (Page 55) |
| Cue 41 | **Richard**: "Let's go to bed ... "<br>*Slowly bring up sound of laboured breathing of a dying man* | (Page 65) |
| Cue 42 | **Cressida** regains control<br>*Fade breathing sound* | (Page 65) |

| | | |
|---|---|---|
| Cue 43 | **Cressida**: " ... keep away, please keep away ... "<br>*Slowly bring up sound of laboured breathing* | (Page 67) |
| Cue 44 | **Cressida**: "You can hear it?"<br>*Increase volume of breathing sound* | (Page 67) |
| Cue 45 | **Richard**: " ... let it pass ... "<br>*Cut breathing sound* | (Page 67) |
| Cue 46 | **Emily** (*off*): "Life is but a dream ... "<br>*Bring up sound of cold wind* | (Page 68) |
| Cue 47 | **Emily**: " — life is but a — dream."<br>*Fade cold wind sound* | (Page 69) |
| Cue 48 | **Richard**: " — what do you think you're ——?"<br>*Bell rings incessantly* | (Page 69) |
| Cue 49 | **Emily** fires the gun<br>*Surreal, echoing acoustic* | (Page 69) |
| Cue 50 | **Cressida** rushes on upstage<br>*Cut bell sound* | (Page 69) |
| Cue 51 | **Cressida**: "Will you please return this?"<br>*Three thuds from the door knocker* | (Page 70) |
| Cue 52 | **Cressida**: "Oh, Richard ..."<br>*Another three thuds* | (Page 70) |
| Cue 53 | **Aubrey** coughs<br>*"The Emperor Waltz" plays; cut when ready* | (Page 71) |
| Cue 54 | Lights fade to black-out<br>*Bring up sound of cold wind; fade slowly when ready* | (Page 73) |